The Anchored Team Process

Navigating & thriving amidst life's storms

Joshua Holloway

Copyright © 2022 Joshua Holloway

The Anchored Team Process: Navigating & thriving amidst life's storms by Joshua Holloway

All rights reserved. This book or any parts thereof may not be reproduced in any manner whatsoever without prior written permission of the author, except in the case of brief quotations embodied in critical articles and reviews or as permitted by U.S. copyright law. For permissions, email the author: jholloway@opendoor406.com

Published by Joshua Holloway
www.opendoor406.com

Front cover design by Creative Nomads
Editing by Kelani Daniels
Workbook design by Christianna Kruger

ISBN: 979-8-9862827-0-1

First printing edition 2022 in the United States

Disclaimers

Legal mumbo jumbo:

So here we go! Reading and working through this workbook in no way signifies that we're in a therapeutic relationship. I believe that the information you'll find in the following pages can and has helped many. However, it's in no way a substitute for professional help. The truth of the matter is, this book will surface thoughts and feelings about yourself and the world you're in, but it's designed to do so in conjunction with a therapist as a guide.

This applies to therapists as well! It's common for us therapists to think we don't need mental health support and that we're capable of healing ourselves. We can't. The basis of the Anchored Team Process is completely centered on the development of a team. This workbook is for educational purposes only, and can be used as a guide to the Anchored (ATP) model of care. If you're ready to drop anchor, take inventory, and prep your ship to finally obey your chosen direction, read on! But do not cowboy/cowgirl this thing y'all! Love you all!

Spiritual mumbo jumbo:

I am a man who professes that Jesus Christ is my Lord and Savior. There are many areas of this workbook that will refer to spiritual principles of the Christian faith that reflect mine and my wifes beliefs. While I in no way desire to impose my faith in Jesus Christ on you, I do encourage you to be honest if you have spiritual wounds. There are no perfect church congregations, and I've seen many people throughout my years as a therapist with church wounds, so let's talk about them!

For the sake of simplicity and staying in my lane of understanding, I don't go into other faith models. This is not to shame or separate; rather, this is due to being true to myself.

Many faith models are solely focused on helping us be better humans. I do operate from the basis that all of us have a spiritual component to us. Holistic treatment from a wellness model incorporates mind, body, and spirit. People refer to this in different ways, and I strongly suggest for you to find the way you understand it. Likewise, I'm always open to sharing where my hope comes from if you want to or are willing to hear it!

- Joshua Holloway, Author

Email list mumbo jumbo:

All of the online forms in this book require an email for two reasons. First, it's a way for you to get a copy of your responses sent to you. Second, we're building an email list to further send resources out like newsletters, mental and medical tips, blog posts, announcements of events and more! If you so desire, there is a way to unsubscribe from the list, but we would love to see you stay!

- Kyle Pettis, Open Door IT Expert

Acknowledgements

I want to take a second and thank my core team, without whom this workbook would not be a reality. Athena, my wife, the love of my life, you allowed me countless late nights and gave me grace through the years putting all of this together! Thanks baby!

Dean, Morgan, Eliza and Josiah Holloway! You're the coolest kids ever! You gave me hope during the tough times, telling me I could do it! You looked at pages of books without pictures and just showed interest in me as your old man! I love you all! Thank you for being an inspiration to me!

Jim, Lee, Lloyd, Mark, Gloire and Dean! You gents have helped me stay in the fight and press into my personal pain. This book started first and foremost with my team and myself! A man could ask for none better!

Kelani, Christianna, Kyle! You all played a major role in helping this come to reality! You all rock! Here's to many more books to come!

New City Church family, thank you for helping me to recharge week after week through ups and downs! Love you all!

Lastly, to our readers! I can only imagine the many people that have read portions of this book, contributed to the stories and poured out hours of their lives to make this happen! You are the most important ones of all! You ROCK!

We all hope and pray that this book changed your life, because it has changed ours!

-Joshua Holloway

Introduction

You are amazing, and I commend you for choosing to work on yourself. It's very likely you don't feel amazing right now, and that's ok! We all have times in our lives where we find ourselves without the answers to our issues. The goal of the Anchored Process is to equip you with the steps to discover these answers.

Throughout this workbook you will see the Anchored Process referred to as the A-Team Process, ATP, and the Anchored Process. These are one in the same.

S.E.G.W.A.Y-

Strengthen, Educate, and Graduate Willing Adults and Youth

During the events of September 11, 2001, I was a young airman. The world as America had known it changed, and fear had taken hold, but unity pulled America together as a team and stood strong.

When I was traveling home after being away for over a year, I first saw a Segway® scooter (a self-balancing, two-wheeled transportation device)[1] at an airport. That Segway® stood for much more than just a means of getting from one place to another-it stood for safety. To me, that Segway® represented the fact that we were not giving up, and that we would not stand down. We in fact were, and would continue, to segue, which refers to transitioning without interruption from one activity or place to another smoothly[2], regardless of circumstances!

It was eleven years later as I worked on my thesis, attempting to develop the origins of this very program, that I was reminded of both the Segway® and the verb "segue". The program was being created to address the needs of at-risk youth in rural Montana and children affected by "ACE" (Adverse Childhood Experiences). To establish the mission for the program, I combined the Segway® Device and the concept of segueing, to get people unstuck and moving from one place to another with as little effort as possible. This birthed the acronym S.E.G.W.A.Y. (Strengthen, Educate, and Graduate Willing Adults and Youth). Words are powerful, so please take a second and really contemplate these two definitions- how they work together and what they convey. Also, let's take a quick moment to ponder:

How would your life be impacted if you left the old thing pulling you down and found a segue to achieve your goals?

S.E.G.W.A.Y. was the prototype for the A-Team Process, which is set around a one-year timeline and is designed to help you segue your life!

We'll now take a look at the therapy process for a couple named Fred and Rita, whose full story you can find in the Anchored novel (which is projected to release in late 2022). While Fred and Rita are representative of real people and circumstances, the specifics of their circumstances are a story all of their own.

I believe we can honestly all find ourselves in some aspects of their story. For those of you who are participating in the workbook portion after reading Anchored, the novel please don't breeze over these areas, as you'll be able to see how the A-Team Process is applied in the lives of Fred, Rita, and their family. As you see the intensity of their struggles and how they're able to overcome using the techniques you'll learn about, my hope is that you'll gain a greater understanding of how you too can overcome.

Fred and Rita

Fred and Rita, a couple in their mid 30's, came to my office one afternoon. Fred, a man with very distinguishable characteristics, sporting a messy work shirt, stained jeans and work boots, expressed without mincing words that he need not stay in my office if he didn't like the way the conversation went. Rita, a petite woman in scrubs in her mid 30's, expressed that she was at her wit's end. She was a healthcare provider and a mom of three (June-13, John-7, and Jude-2). The children were in the waiting room with them at the clinic, sitting between their parents, and all three of them showed little to no emotion. On the outside, they appeared to be extremely well-behaved.

I began the session by asking the familiar question: "What brings you in to see me today?". Rita motioned to Fred for him to answer. As Fred began to speak, we were almost immediately interrupted by June. Without acknowledging anyone in the room other than her mother, she said, "Jude needs a diaper change". Rita got up and flew to the aid of her child as if in a frantic emergency. Fred looked at me with apathy and motioned his hands as if he himself had been thrown to the side while expressing himself. Mom changed the baby, apologizing profusely afterward for the interruption. They both looked at me eagerly, and I asked them how often they felt at peace. They looked with amazement and said, "Peace!?".

That day, we'd end up seeing a common downfall that so many couples face: being surrounded by people all the time, but feeling alone. In fact, during the course of their marriage, Rita had often mentioned wanting a divorce. This wasn't because she wanted to separate from her husband or raise her children on her own, but because she could not continue to parent and support her family "alone". Both spouses expressed loneliness and fear of not knowing what to do next.

Over the next few chapters, you'll see the rest of Fred and Rita's story unfold. The first step to their healing was entering my office, while your first step may very well come through finishing this book. Regardless, stay in the fight!

Chapter 1:
Empowerment

The A-Team Process (ATP) is a systematic, action-oriented therapeutic model. It's a demanding model that requires a lot of action on your part, but if you're willing to put in the work, your life can change dramatically over a one-year period of time. The best part is that you're not doing this alone. Many hands make light work! We ease you in, and help you develop the skills one step at a time. Together we can empower you and accomplish so much! Empowerment is the name of the game, and reconciliation (as far as we can take it together) is the vehicle for change. First and foremost, we start with understanding our memory and how that memory affects us. Secondly, we reconcile with those involved in our story. We provide you the empowerment to confront even those who've hurt you. Don't worry! This isn't something you do on your own!

We help you confront (in a safe way, surrounded by a team) through our process called "empty chair and an invitation". Empty chair is a technique that's been in therapy for many generations, originally developed by Fritz Perls, and is used today in a form of therapy called Gestalt Therapy. We combine Empty Chair with an invite in a rather powerful and impactful way. In chapter 6, we'll go more into detail about what this process involves.

During this year, you'll learn to get in the driver's seat of your life-a spot so many people forfeit. Being in the driver's seat requires focus and attention. It requires more from you than when you "back seat it" and allow someone or something else to take over. We "back seat" our lives when we allow things like alcohol, drugs, sex, pornography, gaming, work, Netflix, social media, our children-pick your poision-to take over.

Fred and Rita took a back seat to their children, careers, alcohol, and pornography, all in an attempt to "cope". This method of coping, however, sent their lives into an uncontrollable tailspin (as coping always does). Coping is not actually living, it's pseudo-living. It's a pseudo (fake) substitute in its inability to produce long term sustainable outcomes. Coping may work short-term, but fails us in the long haul.

Chapter 2:
Equipping

Starting this process will require a little bit of self-examination. You'll need to decide for yourself that it's time to end the CHAOS: Choices, Honesty, Acceptance, Ownership, Stewardship.

Choices: Before you can begin ATP, you have to come to terms with your choices. You have to ask yourself, "Am I stuck?", and "When did that (insert vice of choice) run my life into the ditch?"

Honesty: It's important to be honest with yourself during this process. You're going to confront hard things in your life, but it's key that you decide you are worth the work, and that you can let another person into your life. Other people in your life can't be the only ones who think you're worth it-you have to know you're worth it too!

Acceptance: Accept that there are things in your life that have happened to you, and there aren't always simple explanations as to why they happened. Regardless, no amount of explanations can change what happened. We must, however, understand that these things did occur, and NOT run from the pain, embrace it!

"You can't make sense out of the senseless. You will only lose who you

are, even after losing who you were." - Joshua Holloway

Ownership: Taking ownership isn't popular, but it's a key component in your healing journey! No one, and I mean no one, has ever made a choice for you. Even if someone threatened you at gunpoint, there is still a choice: do what they're telling you or get shot. It's time you tell that old self to pound sand- your choices are your own again.

Stewardship: Now, it's time to be intentional about handling issues in your life. In the words of the music group Incubus: *will you choose to drive?*

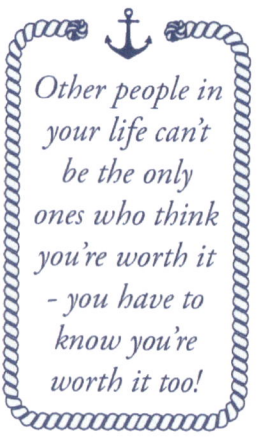

Other people in your life can't be the only ones who think you're worth it - you have to know you're worth it too!

We often slide into the back seat and hand the control of our lives over to someone or something else. This is when true chaos ensues. Chaos is defined as "complete disorder and confusion"[3]. While the previously mentioned list (see chap 1) is not an exhaustive one, who/what we allow to drive our minds, thoughts, and emotions has control over us, thus producing chaos.

Many of us react with anger and defensiveness when beginning to confront things in our lives. This is denial, which is defined as "the action of declaring something to be untrue"[4]. We look shocked when someone points out how we are not in control and we often attack them verbally, emotionally and sometimes even physically.

Sliding into the back seat is such a temptation because it brings instant relief. However, much like a nerve blocker (a numbing of a limb for a surgical procedure), the pain is really still there, and often comes back with a vengeance. Taking the back seat looks different for everyone, but now you have your first opportunity to "be an investigator of your past"! You have the opportunity to take the power back!

Take a look at the CHAOS model and evaluate your choices, honor, acceptance, ownership, and stewardship. Evaluating your personal CHAOS will help you take back control and get out of that back seat.

C: Choices

H: Honor

A: Acceptance

O: Ownership

S: Stewardship

You can begin the CHAOS process by defining specific vices in your life. A vice is defined as immoral or wicked behavior. It's something that grips to hold something in place. Your vice is that thing that draws you and offers you happiness and tranquility. It delivers for a moment in time, but then leaves you having to do one of two things: embrace the suck or consume the vice.

Note that we're not just talking about addictive substances here. The vice could be a process (lying, stealing, gossiping, gambling) or a substance (alcohol, illicit drugs, abused prescription medications).

Your Who: The person(s) who first exposed you to the vice or created the circumstance for access. For example: an older sibling who leaves a pornographic magazine lying around, or a friend who offers to lie for you.

Your What: This is the circumstance that led to first encounter with the vice. For instance: you were drinking, and that's when you hit someone. This is also looked at as the chain of events leading to the first exposure (see Joshua and Athena's stories in the following sections).

Your When: This is the age you were when exposed. For example: drinking at a funeral at the age of 7.

Your Where: Exactly as it sounds. Where did the first exposure of the vice happen? For instance: at an office party.

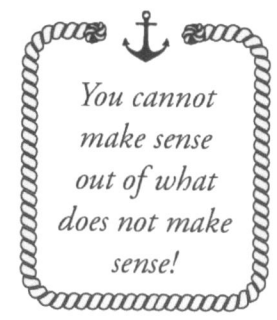

You cannot make sense out of what does not make sense!

Your How: This is a detailed account of first use. These details will be used later in the development of your story!

I want to conclude with one area that many have asked about. Why isn't there a "why"? That is because it truly doesn't matter. We can so easily get stuck here. The "why" is a trap. Avoid it! It only leads to bitterness, guilt, and shame. We dive into the "why" only in the present, because that we can impact, but never the past! You cannot make sense out of what does not make sense!

In the lines below, take some time to write down your vice and the who, what, when, and where that caused it to come into your life.

Vice:

Who:

What:

When:

Where:

How:

Athena's Vice Process

When I asked my wife, Athena, to write down her vice, she felt that there were too many to write down just one! She chose to write down marijuana, and here's what it looked like in her life:

Vice: *Marijuana*

Who: *Sibling*

What: *Since I had been drinking before I used, I ended up feeling* way more drunk and blurry. Eventually, as some of you might know... I got the munchies and ate a bunch of junk food at my brother's house.

When: *12 yrs old*

Where: *Outside of the Silver Spur Bar in Vaughn, MT*

How: *I had been drinking beer and when people around me were using it and one person asked me if I wanted to try and I said yes. I wanted to be cool. I wanted to be accepted. I was the only girl in my family.*

As a result of this, I handed control of my life over to people's approval. Drugs and alcohol also sent me down a spiral. Later, I thought, "My brothers would have been perfectly fine if I didn't want to try it". However, I made a choice to get in the back seat and no longer drive.

My whole sphere of influence in my life at that time changed. I started hanging around people who were engaged in similar activities. I'm not attempting to shame or guilt anyone, just state the facts. It was my normal. I love my family dearly and wouldn't trade them for the world, but we put the "fun" in dysfunctional!

What did this vice do in my life? This led me to legal issues, medical issues, mental health issues, and a struggle that has still crept up from time to time.

Joshua's Vice Process

Vice: *Food*

Who: *My biological father left. I honestly recall several times just* wanting to cope.

What: *Food addiction as a medicine. I wanted two things every day: McDonalds before being dropped off, and a soda while I was at daycare.*

When: *I believe I was 4-5.*

Where: *Being dropped off at daycare.*

How: *I would beg for a Happy Meal, which I truly recall in my head thinking would not have been enough food (that was untrue) but like all vices you have to do more, consume more, enact more each time to achieve the desired chemical responses. Thus is unsustainable.*

Here's what's crazy about this story. Like so many of us, I had a person attempt to help me with something I didn't even understand to be an issue. I don't know his name, nor can I recall his face, so I'll just refer to him as John.

John was the manager of the daycare. At that time in my family's life, I recall that we were often poor, sometimes living with my grandmother or another family member. I remember my mother working hard and working often (which unfortunately caused me to form an unhealthy relationship with food).

John, at that time, became my person. At Open Door (and even in my family home), we often use the statement "people are people". A person is a person, and to allow another person control over your life is codependency or enmeshment. Neither of these are healthy. On the contrary, allowing a person to have influence in your life is quite the opposite:

Control: To have power over.[5]

Influence: the act or power of producing an effect without apparent exertion of force or direct exercise of command.[6]

John was my main go-to for getting my soda money (#80's baby). But the problem was, my mom never left money with him. These exchanges would go somewhat like this…

"Mr. John"

"Yes Joshua".

"I really want a soda. Can I have my money to get one?"

"I am sorry Joshua, you don't have any soda money today"

"Oh no… I am thirsty".

"You don't need to drink soda if you are thirsty, but you can grab some water back there. It's probably better for you anyway".

"But I don't like water. Can I borrow the money for a soda?"

"Alrighty, I will let you borrow the money for a soda," he would relent, handing me a quarter.

Internally, I'd be running and shouting! Woohoo! I repeated this pattern for days. I'm not sure exactly how long until the fateful day came when I learned two lessons:

1. Money borrowed is money owed.
2. I didn't need a soda every day (even though I really wanted one).

I can only imagine my mother's surprise when Mr. John asked her to settle for my tab. My soda train had come to an end. Mr. John cared for me, and in the end he became a man who impacted my life drastically. We talked to my mom together. I had a choice then and there, to embrace my CHAOS and work through it or repeat the pattern. I can say I learned some of that lesson but not all.

I learned that a person had to pay their way, and that stuck with me. I can remember thinking that many times. This may have actually kicked my little brain into entrepreneur mode. I recall many times as an adult thinking if I wanted something, I needed to find a way to make it happen!

Consequences are neither good nor bad, they just are!

What didn't stick in my mind was my unhealthy relationship with food. This has been a weak area of my life ever since. That's the thing about our vices... we can hand back the wheel (take the back seat) whenever we want. Driving and back-seating both have consequences. Consequences are neither good nor bad, they just are!

What are we willing to live with? In my case, missing out on the feelings that I get when I eat or drink something tasty, or taking care of my body? I can say I have lived in both. Please give your vice exercise the time and attention it deserves. This exercise is key and oftentimes you will find that there is more than one vice. That's okay!! Go through this vice process for each one in your life. It will pay off!

Chapter 3:
Enlistment

As we've discussed, while it's often easier to shift to the back seat of our lives, it takes us out of the driver's seat. It's time to step up and "spite the vice"! Don't allow other people or things to run your life because you don't want someone else controlling your life!

Stepping up to your vice is self-leadership, and this is where the real work begins. Self-leadership is the point where you put a stop to your CHAOS. By doing this, you can allow a person into your life, not for control, but rather for influence. Are you willing to enlist the help of others to influence your life? If so, drop anchor and let's get started!

It's time to step up and "spite the vice"!

Identifying your vice and your who, what, when, and where is the beginning of your Anchored Process. Then, at a certain point in your journey, you will enlist the help of a team to get you going!

1st Quarter: 3 months

Intensive weekly therapy: Research shows that weekly sessions provide the needed inertia to succeed, so the first three months of ATP implements weekly therapy sessions. Our process centers around REAL (Reality,

Encouragement, Acceptance, Leadership) change, and in each session, evaluate the following areas:

Reality: *Folks, the garbage is what it is.*

Encouragement: *The truth is, we don't have to settle for the garbage.*

Acceptance: *We accept the garbage as something we can't change.*

Leadership: *We take out the garbage we can change.*

Earn your therapy "Book It" stars: There are a handful of books assigned during this process. Each of these must be read prior to the first team meeting.

- *Gap and Gain* by Dan Sullivan
- *Extreme Ownership* by Jocko Willink and Leif Babin
- *Suffering* by Paul David Tripp
- *The Goal* by Eliyahu M. Goldratt
- *Atomic Habits* by James Clear
- *Leadership Pain: The Classroom for Growth* by Samuel R. Chand

Write your story: If it happened to you, through you, or around you, it's a part of you. You'll create your story in a Google Doc (more on this later). You can also head to opendoor406.com/materials and click on "Life Story" to work on your story via an interactive Google form.

Life-Storying: The Foundation of ATP

List of Players: If a person has impacted you positively or negatively, he or she has a role in your life and makes your players list!

Timeline: Chronological organization is key, it helps the readers (your team, and whoever else you allow in your circle to understand flow) see your life unfold. It also defrags your harddrive!

Writing the story: Satisfying on so many levels, very difficult on others. This story you will work on forever- never forget it's not done until you are.

Prep and recruit your team members: Having and utilizing the people in your life is important for this process. We can help you figure out who they are and enlist them as TEAM members:

Teach: Perspectives are powerful, and there is wisdom with much counsel. Each TEAM member has a role and will be called upon to share their insight and teach those around them, from the youngest to the oldest member!

Expectations: We all have expectations! Expectations are "a strong belief that something will happen or be the case in the future." [7] We are personally responsible for our expectations. The closer the relationship, the stronger the connection, the more expectations.

"Un-met uncommunicated expectations lead to premeditated resentments". - Nicole McAdam, former partner and wonderful friend

Acceptance: There are some things we cannot change. We often fight, deny, or run from these things. The Anchored Process requires that we fully embrace and forgive to find true freedom.

Management: We must own that we are in control of our destination. What we've put in has been the catalyst of the outcome we currently reside in.

"Here is the great thing! If you have breath you can change it! If you don't have breath you don't care anymore." - Joshua Holloway

2nd Quarter: 3 Months

Gel as a team: Groups/tribes take time and intentionality to cultivate. Your TEAM is asked to give a one-year commitment of monthly meetings. The TEAM meeting consists of a 2-hour initial meeting, followed by 1.5-hour meetings monthly for 12 months. Each member on your team will also have an ATP workbook and will have their own steps they will adhere to. We will assist you all in this!

TEAM members are asked to fully buy in to helping you! The reality that many therapists understand is that when we help others, we learn as much (if not more) than we teach! I have never had a TEAM member that didn't say they felt like they got way more out of the process than anyone else!

Sharing your story: Sharing your story is preparation for REALLY sharing your story. You have a choice of whether you grow or don't grow. Growth comes from discomfort, and discomfort is uncomfortable. This is where the rubber meets the road and you begin your true freedom journey.

To begin writing your story, use the acronym SHARE: Still, Harness, Acceptance, REAL (therapy), Execute the SHAREs.

Still: Sitting in and embracing your pain can be very trying at times. Being still is something that pulls us out of fight, flight, or freeze, which are common trauma responses. We want you to embrace your suck!

Harness: Take hold of the power of "we" and having a TEAM. Embrace the fact that you can't change without us. We are referring to harness in the literal sense. We work in connection with others, and I have many times attempted to help a person gain understanding here by putting on a literal harness.

Attaching yourself to a structure has consequences. Consequences vary, and are neither good nor bad. Harnessing up and attaching yourself slows you down, and at times you lose mobility. This is a beautiful thing!

I want to illustrate this point further with a story. A hotel was being built in Great Falls, MT, the city where Open Door has it's main headquarters. I would drive everyday and see people working around six or seven stories up. There were poles every 10-15 feet on this roof, and each person had a lead that was attached to their harness. They would tug, pull, and at times seem very frustrated with these attachments. However, no one was working without their harness attached!

The harnesses can feel annoying and feel like overkill 90% of the time. Your team may feel similar at first. In the end, the harness can save your life, so having that annoying attachment makes all the pain and frustration worth it! Similarly, buckle up and strap in! You may undoubtedly fall, but the question is: do you want to smack the ground or have to occasionally pull some slack in your line?

Acceptance: You cannot change or control the past- you can only change and control your actions.

REAL: Therapy with a purpose.

Execute: Kill that controller and take back your power!

1. Share with your therapist
2. Share with your closest peer
3. Share with your team
4. Share with whoever it can help!

3rd Quarter: 3 Months

Continue skills learned in previous quarters.

You are a product of the time you spend on you, physically, spiritually, and mentally. The work you have or have not put in is giving you the results you desire. There's a phrase that says, "You get out of it what you put into it". If you find that you're not who or where you want to be, then end the CHAOS. When we live in chaos, we find we typically weigh ourselves on one end or the other, relying too much on professionals when we don't have quality support in our lower levels!

This quarter is all about the solidification of a team, consisting of your peer, mentor and spiritual support. You'll share your story with them, looping them into the process. You will seek insight and help as you learn to trust and hope in people again. The goal here is to finish strong, by doing the prep work for the final stage.

"Give me six hours to chop down a tree and I will spend the first four sharpening the axe." -Abraham Lincoln

Think of the 3rd Quarter as sharpening the axe.

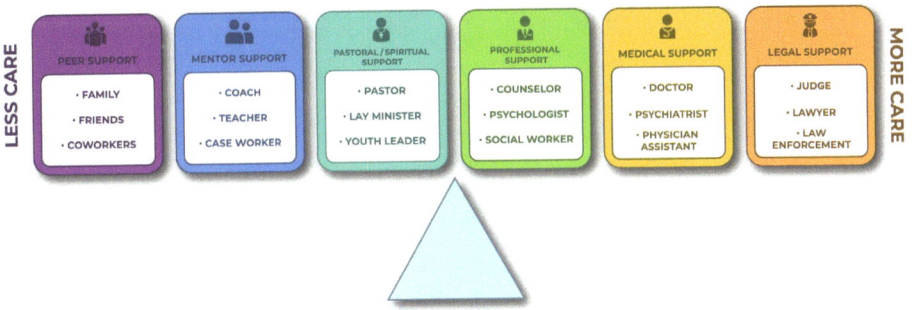

4th Quarter: 3 months

Continue skills learned in previous quarters.

To follow up with Abe's quote, the 4th quarter is where we chop down the tree. This is where ALL (Aligned Life & Liberty) the prep work begins to shine. This is where ALL of your work comes together. True alignment removes cognitive dissonance. We like to say "dissonance is cool in jazz, but horrific and controlling when in thoughts and behaviors". You are more confident and beginning to form relationships that will forever change your life.

Goals for the 4th quarter are:

1. Instill hope.
2. Transition from a lone survivor to a goal-oriented thriver.
3. Have an understanding of the pain in your past.
4. With the love and support of your team to confront those who have hurt you in the past
5. Once and for all, clear out the closet!

Complete the workbook, and graduate ATP. We encourage you to in effort to continue in that selflessness to find a person to be a peer, mentor and spiritual guide for!

Chapter 4:
Enlargement

The phases of the program follow the acronym STRESS (Stuck, Team, Recruiting, Excitement, Strengthen, Success). The phases of STRESS are defined as follows:

Stuck: This is where we all have to be to truly desire and seek change. We must feel as if we have no option but to change. Stuck is where you begin to write your story.

There is a common phrase used in the Anchored Process that says "embrace the suck!" The SUCK is truly what get's you un-stuck! People attempt to escape pain, and many of us avoid it or run from it. The underlying cause for the vast majority of pain is, in fact, the avoidance of pain. When you're stuck and you acknowledge and accept it, the process of change can begin!

Team: This will consist of a person in each of these roles: peer, mentor, spiritual, professional, medical, and legal. Don't worry if you can't think of any names yet-you and your therapist will solve this together. If you know who they are or who you want to ask, write them below!

Peer:

Mentor:

Spiritual:

Professional:

Medical:

Legal:

Recruiting your team: Who do you want in your world? Why do you want them there? What do they bring to your world? When can you next ask them to be a part of your team? Recruiting involves the right team members being in their right places, with the fluidity for that to change (as roles always do!).

Excitement: Most of us have heard the phrase "Strike while the iron is hot". Truth be told, if you aren't feeling hopeful with having people surrounding you who are rooting for your success, we may need to have your medical team member check your pulse!

Strengthen: Check out our Open Door blog to learn mental health skills that will take you less than a minute a week to implement. Practice the skills a lot and do so each day if you want optimal results! A minute a week to a better you!

Success: With these pieces in place, you can tackle anything! Strength comes from many hands working together to accomplish the same goal!

Leaving the basics

Maslow's hierarchy of needs is a great and widely accepted understanding of what our basic needs are and, in a simplified way, how we seek to fulfill those needs. We see these things played out in our everyday lives. At times we see them expressed in small ways, and at other times, larger and much more detrimental ways.

For example, a physiological need we all have is the need to breathe. A person who is drowning and without air (our most very basic need) may panic, and this can cause them to harm or pull under the person attempting to help them. These are basic survival instincts, which cause our more formative thought portions of our brain to, in effect, shut down. Without cause and effect thought processes we miss very important details, such as the fact that a person can't save us if we don't let them.

Just know that a person in a mental health crisis or "survival mode" will often do many things to derail the helping process. This is where I recommend creating a safe word to give to your teams.

The purpose of this word would be to let your team know that you need a break from the process for a time, with the intention of continuing it later. This word is a cue for safety and security; a cease-fire. My wife and I have one ourselves when we're working through issues!

Anyone can call the safe word! Sometimes, your team may see that you need a break in the process even if you don't. In the Anchored novel, you will see this play out in Fred and Rita's story on several occasions.

Think here for a minute and pinpoint your position on "Maslow's

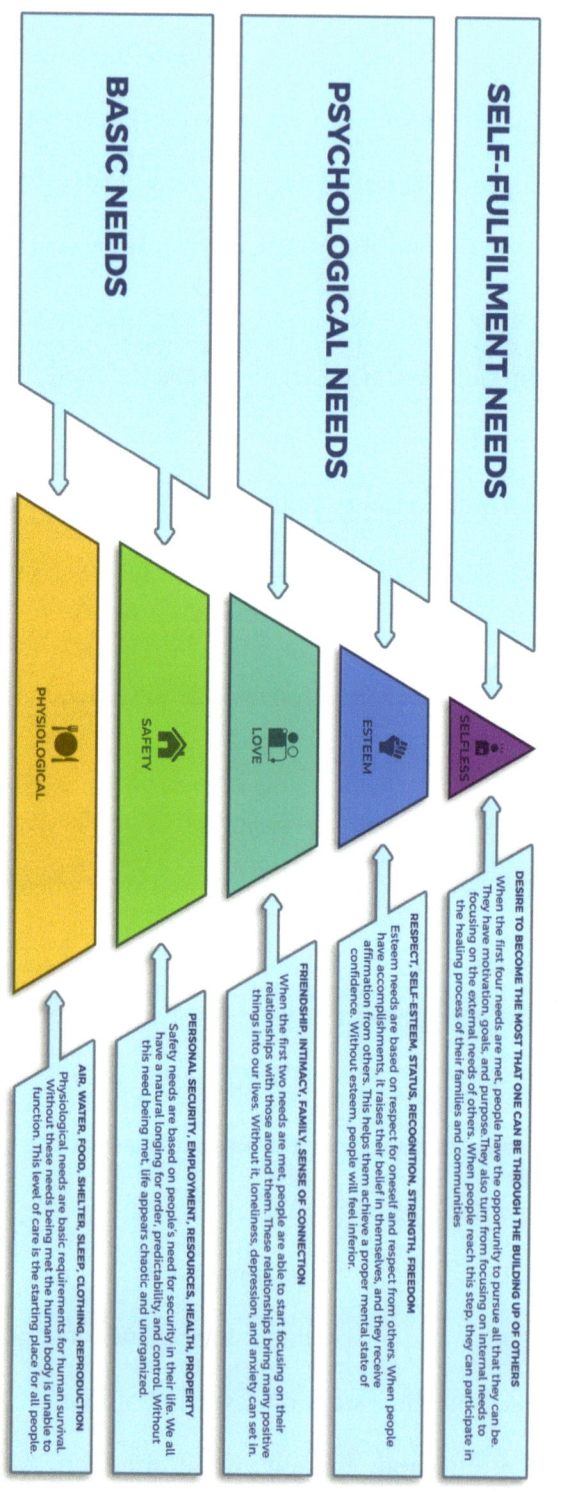

Hierarchy of Needs". Give yourself space to be honest about your needs, be they high- or low-level! Knowing where you are is important simply because you can see potential pitfalls associated with the different levels! The pitfalls for the levels are:

Physiological: When you can't breathe you do not care about safety. For example, if you're scuba diving in the ocean and your girlfriend or boyfriend broke up with you, that's all you'd be able to think about as you look at the beautiful coral reef. Then you get bumped by a shark and lose your air tank (which you neglected to secure due to thinking about your love life). In that moment, what are you worrying about, breathing or sharks? You are worrying about breathing. Questions to consider:

- Do you have adequate access to the most basic of needs?
    - Food
    - Water
    - Air

Safety: Once you can breathe then you start locating the shark. You are trying to get distance and protect yourself. You leave the gear at the bottom of the sea, knowing you'll have to pay for it (you're broke, but you're not thinking about that right now). Questions to consider now:

- Are you able to sleep soundly?
    - Home (can be an apartment, house, mobile home).
    - Clothing that is clean and adequate.
    - Feeling free from daily fear.

Love: Once you are out of the water, in the boat and safe, you thank God above that you are alive. Now you think about your boy/girlfriend, mom, dad, and sister (knowing you were upset with most of them before but none of that matters now). Questions to consider here:

- With most basic needs met, do you have a person you feel close to that understands you, and truly listens?
    - Have a person who calls/texts you regularly?
    - Someone at least once a week that says hello or engages with you kindly?
    - A person you desire to be close to on a regular basis that also desires to be close to you?

Esteem: You now seek out connection with your family and girl/boyfriend, their response (for example caring for you and listening) will encourage both of you to enter the final level. Questions to consider now:

- Do you feel as if you can positively influence those around you or your environment?
    - Can you help a person meet his or her neeeds?
    - Can you reach out to someone when you think of them?
    - Do you actually do those things mentioned above?

Selfless: Selflessness leads to selflessness. If you were heard when you were attacked by the shark then you will likely be able to focus on others more easily. This also all contributes to our stages of a relationship mentioned throughout ATP! Questions to consider:

- Can you do all of the things above in the other tiers when you do not feel like it?
    - Do you actually do those things?

Chapter 5:
Encouragement

So back to Fred and Rita. Fred was, by all means, what many would refer to as "a man's man". Therapy was not his idea of help. In fact, by his own admission, he said from the beginning that he rarely, if ever, asked for help. Being willing to come to therapy was by all means a last ditch effort.

This "man's man" was not leading his family in any way. He deferred the leadership to anyone who was willing to take it. He hid in hard work, alcohol and pseudo-relationships that surrounded those activities. Fred stood about 6'2" and had a chiseled jaw and a handshake that would crush a walnut. He had a fun and happy-go-lucky demeanor, but in moments of quiet or when he thought no one was looking, held a genuine look of concern or sadness in his face and in his stance.

Fred and Rita regularly attended and were involved in their church, serving in various roles as they were asked. Fred would often lament to those that would ask about his sad looks that he had no one who was really there for him. Strangely, there were always people who reached out through their small group or even through work, asking him for help and expressing the desire to get to know him better. He was a brilliant mechanic and never met a problem he couldn't solve (professionally speaking).

Rita was a caregiver by nature. She was a woman who loved to serve her family, friends, and her church. Giving of herself and busyness was her way of coping, because as we'll discover later in the story, she had unacknowledged and undealt with trauma.

She loved everyone, and yet expressed about two months after coming to therapy that she really could not think of anyone she trusted. She came to a point where she felt she could finally trust someone, and that someone was me–a professional counselor, and by all means a person she was paying to be there for her. It was disheartening to her that the only person she could trust was a stranger whom she was paying. Truth be told, this is a sentiment shared by many people who seek out therapeutic services. I can't count how many times people have said, "I just wish I could trust (insert name here) the way I trust you", and Rita was no exception.

This couple was experiencing broken trust, hurt, and trauma that altered their lives. Both Fred and Rita had experiences with trauma. They were very different experiences, as trauma varies from person to person, and their stories highlight these differences.

Let's look at Fred and Rita's stuck/suck process:

Fred was controlled by his mother after the death of his father at the age of fifteen. His mom's fear caused Fred to allow others to drive for him. The death of his dad, while hard, was not traumatic for him. He missed and loved his dad, but his mother was petrified of losing her only son. His parents had a loving relationship, but she never allowed herself to grieve (more on this later).

Rita was raped in high school by a young man she was previously attracted to. While attending a ball game as a high school cheerleader, he raped her on the bus ride home. She was asleep when this happened. Petrified, Rita froze and said nothing, pretending to still be asleep. After the bus ride, Rita pulled aside both her coach and the football coach, who was a man she had looked up to. These were two people who typically did not put up with nonsense. When she told them, they seemed genuinely concerned. Both coaches appeared to take her seriously and immediately took her to the hospital.

That night changed her life forever. Subtle things that others said about this situation made Rita feel as if there was little seriousness to the crime that had taken place. She felt as if she was alone. The coaches believed her, but appeared to just want the issue to go away. Honestly, so did she. After that night she never spoke of what had taken place until she had been drinking or was extremely angry. While Rita attempted to hide how she felt, it would only push her deeper and deeper into a tenacious self-reliance. The hospital administered the Plan-B pill as a precaution, and Rita struggled for years over feelings of loneliness and regret.

She never shared the story after that night and attempted to pretend that the rape never occured. Often, when she was approached by her parents and fellow students, who could tell something was different, she would make up an excuse on the fly. For many years, she was thought of as flaky, which is something that couldn't be further from the truth. She blamed herself, always questioning why this happened, and wondered if she'd ever feel normal again.

Rita dropped out of all extra curricular activities and started working. She began saving, graduated early, and looked from the outside like a driven and determined young lady. She did all of this in an effort to never appear flaky again, as she discovered that if she were committed, people would understand all the things she said "no" to. She went to school, earned a 4.0, became a nurse, and eventually began a career as a nurse practitioner. By all standards, she was successful.

While in therapy, she opened up for the first time since the night she told her coaches what had happened. This was the beginning of allowing her circle to grow, with me, her therapist, becoming the first person she trusted.

Rita and Fred gladly assumed their assigned roles. Rita controlled all she could in order to keep her mind off her daily fear and trauma. They were very successful by the world's standards- they had a nice home, lived in the right neighborhood, had retirement taken care of, and had little to no debt. She owned a clinical practice and had her kids in a private school.

Fred and Rita's children being with them in the waiting room at that first visit would become a norm. Rita's fear and Fred's complacency made their family unit rely solely on Rita, as we'll soon see.

Rita and Fred had both entered the clinic in a state we call emotional divorce or separation. This happens in all types of relationships. This takes place when those relationships dip ahead of what is known as the relationship baseline or "status quo" and each person becomes separated from others. One of the saddest truths is that emotional separation or unforgiveness destroys all of our relationships. In this case, Rita's emotional separation from her husband had started years before, after her rape. Fred's emotional separation was tied to his lack of forgiveness with his mother. Undelt with trauma robs us of the connection we need.

Neither Fred or Rita desired emotional separation. Both felt it, but they did not, until our program, have the words to name it nor the tools to battle it. We fight separation with connection. We fight this by partnering as a team!

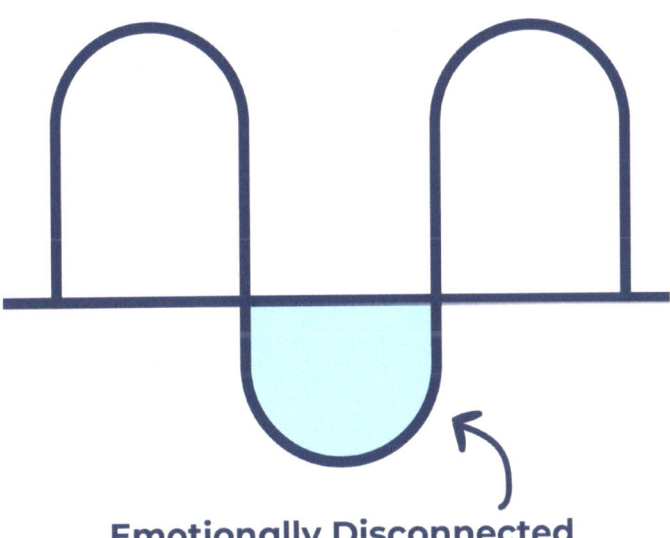

Emotionally Disconnected

When you dip below the relationship baseline or "status quo", you become emotionally disconnected from the other person. It is extemely difficult to reconnect/repair the relationship once it gets to this point.

Chapter 6:
Engagement

Fred and Rita were successful, driven people, raising what many people have referred to as "perfect children". However, they both have trauma.

Do you feel that you align with Fred or Rita? Do you see any similarities in your life?

Define your stuck/suck:

Issues: everyone has them, some are honest about them, few do something about them, even less choose to master them.

What issue(s)has/have control over your life?

GOAL

Grasp: The fact is, this issue has control over you, but you alone are able to give away your control. You have power, you can take back your life by squashing the issue at its core.

Own: Your part. Sometimes you may have a part in this, sometimes you don't. Sort this out with your therapist and team. We may not have had ownership in the originating event, much like Rita. She did nothing to contribute to the original event. Rita took ownership of herself and sought help. Will you?

Accept: The things that you had no control over. Know that they are real, but not current (and if they are current, go back to step 1 and enlist help!).

Let it GO: Forgiveness is the greatest gift you can give yourself.

- Forgiveness: what it is and what it isn't
    - Forgiveness *is* canceling of a debt
    - Forgiveness *is* accepting that what happened is real and was wrong
    - Forgiveness *is* freedom
    - Forgiveness *is not* saying it was or is okay
    - Forgiveness *is not* taking ownership for another person's garbage
    - Forgiveness *is not* accepting that what the other person did was ok
    - Forgiveness *is not* blindly trusting again

- Forgiveness *is not (always)* reconciliation.
    • Reconciliation refers to re-entering into a relationship. While it's great when we can forgive, people still must take ownership for the damage they caused. In some cases it can be unhealthy or unsafe to reconcile a relationship. Talking with your team will be helpful to assess the situation.
• Forgiveness is forgiveness/reconciliation is reconciliation. This is one of the largest concerns with forgiveness.
    - People always wonder, "Will the person hurt me again?" This is a common question. You should never put yourself in harm's way.

What is your primary GOAL?

Remember, the A-Team Process is all about empowerment and reconciliation! We want you to have a team and confront all the things and people in your life that caused harm! This makes them lose their power. This should only be done with a trained and experienced team. The A-Team Process equips you for just that!

There are two outcomes in the ATP:
1. Reconciliation to yourself
2. Reconciliation to others

We help you reconcile, first and foremost, to yourself-to the true you, the empowered you, the fearless two-year-old you! Our goal is to bring you to a place as if you'd never had that abuse/neglect/trauma- we intend on helping make the world small again. We do so through enlarging your sphere of influence. With the right team you can take on the world- your world!

Secondly, we intend to help you confront those that have harmed you emotionally, physically, sexually, etc. We do so through our empty chair and invitation process, which looks something like this:

- A-Team Process
- Team education and preparation
- Decision on timeline to confront once the team is fully up to speed.
- Creation of your specific story, a letter you wish to share with the person(s) who hurt you.
- Reading/sharing that story with the team.
- Filming day!!
  - We have our media team come together and set up the set. We have the empty chair, invitation, and a hope that the person will show up (the in-person invitation goes out two weeks prior with hopes of their attendance.)
- If they show up, we have a session for you to share your thoughts!
- If they don't, we film the empty chair and an invitation!

- Then we send the video and ask them to join.

We do all this to empower you! We believe in you and you can do it! This is a process, one that you will be ready for. It has been said that our process is similar to stirring a hornet's nest, but with a professional beekeeper at your side! Before having your team involved there are many situations that can be terrifying and not smart to take on by yourself! Remember we don't cowboy/cowgirl this thing! We are all better together.

Chapter 7:
Emotional Processing

No matter how many times I've walked people through the requirements of a story, there inevitably are many who struggle getting started. This is usually due to deeper underlying therapeutic issues surrounding perfection, fear of judgment, or shame associated with a person's story. Here's the storying process I like to lead people through:

First things first!
- Create a Google Doc, title it your "Name's life story, Version 1, Year" (i.e. "Josh's Life Story, Version 1, 2022).
- Share the document with your therapist, even if it's blank.

List of Players:
- List people in your life past/present/future (You may be thinking, *future*? This is so incredibly important due to how often we destroy or discredit relationships before they start! Think about your future wife, husband, inlaw, boss, neighbor.)
  - Mom, Dad, Grandma, teachers, Johnny or Suzie down the street, bosses, kids, spouse.

Timeline:

- A birth to current line:
  - Bust out the arts and crafts!
  - A timeline is exactly as it sounds: draw a line and mark important events.
    - Born in 1950, broke leg in 1955, Dad got a promotion, we moved into a beautiful home but had no family around, 1980 bought a Mustang 5.0 (almost killed myself in that car), and so on.
  - Involve family members who are trusted. Include dates and people's names.

To you, through you, or around you:

- If it happened to/through/around you, it's a part of you, and in turn, a part of your story. Leave nothing out.
  - Only you can write your story, only you can share everything! CLEAN OUT THE CLOSET AND LEAVE NOTHING HIDDEN. Anything left hidden will void the process!
  - Jot down the top five things you have never shared with anyone. No one has to see this except your therapist, but writing it here will help you transition it to your timeline and ultimately into your story.

1.
2.
3.
4.
5.

Now we connect the dots and write our story:

- We start with earliest memories
- We leave nothing out
- We differentiate if the piece of our story is something we remember or if it was told to us. For example:
    - I remember breaking my arm falling out of a tree
    - Grandma told me I fell out of the tree and broke my arm.
    - I have pictures of my broken arm at Christmas when I was five but I can't remember it.

This is an ATP participant's guide to addressing issues in their lives, developing their team, executing change, and taking back control in their lives. This will outline the roles and responsibilities and minimum time/participation commitments we ask of our future team. This also gives you a spot to write down questions that you have for the people on your team.

First things first, if you have relationship wounds, then you have experienced breaks in attachment. The diagram ahead addresses a relationship pattern we teach on extensively and refer back to throughout the program. This is a guide to relationship flow, and we put it in at this point in the workbook to give you a guide and a reference point to focus on when times get tough on your team, and folks they will. That doesn't mean you have a bad team, it means PEOPLE ARE PEOPLE. People will mess up, we just have to learn to differentiate between those who intentionally do harm and those who make a mistake! **(We do not excuse abuse! EVER!)**

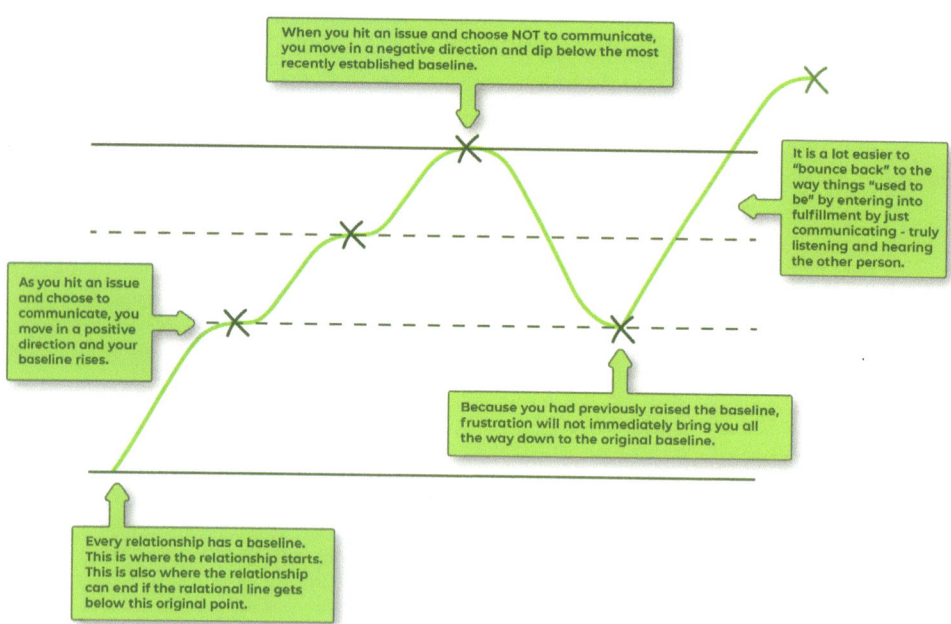

Chapter 8:
Emotionally Connecting with Others

Ask yourself this, "what is encouraging to me?" There are many different things that can embody encouragement. One of the main things that I feel is encouraging is the ability to stick with something. You are 8 chapters into this process! You have thought deeply as you have read and you are embracing the good, the bad and the ugly! You have made a choice to better yourself, and allow a person(s) into your life! Let's face it, you rock!

Be yourself! How to be you:

- Do not censor yourself.
- So often, a person comes into therapy concerned with being judged or shamed. Know that judgment and shame have no place in the therapy process.
- The other side of the coin is that many times a person who is offended or wounded is very sensitive. We will go over questions and look at FIT and delivery later in this workbook! Just know you are in good company if you are sensitive. It means you can still feel!

The self-reliant "superman/superwoman"'s kryptonite is teamwork. We're going to incorporate one person at a time to widen our sphere of influence and help us to continue to make the world small again! We make our world small to control all we can. Unfortunately, this fallacy harms us in many ways, primarily making the world become a very large and scary place, but this does not have to be the case. We can make anyone's world small again by increasing your team!

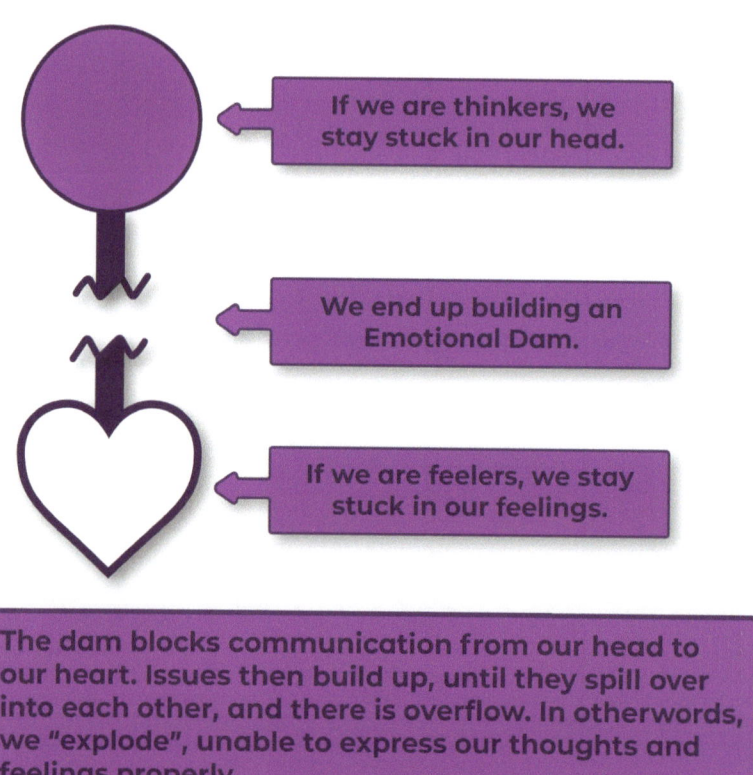

Fred and Rita Continued

At this point in the A-Team Process, Fred and Rita had been attending sessions regularly for nearly three months. Both had produced their first draft for each of their stories. Upon sharing them, they both ended up adding as much as they read over the first few sharing sessions.

5TH RING: MENTOR SUPPORT - This person with always be there, but it may not always be the same person. As you enter different seasons of life, or your needs change, your mentor will change to support those changes.

OUTERMOST RING: PEER SUPPORT - Everyone has peers and everyone needs peers. We should get to a place where we can live in this ring. This is where we are the furthest from ourself and making the most impact on our family, our friends and our community. And ultimately, on ourselves.

INNERMOST CIRCLE: SELF - This is you, wherever you are right now.

2ND RING: THE ENCOURAGER - Who is the person that encouraged you to seek help?

3RD RING: YOUR TEAM (PROFESSIONAL SUPPORT) - This encompasses your team, the people who will help you on your way to health and wholeness. They will not be needed forever, but will be there to provide support.

4TH RING: SPIRITUAL SUPPORT - This is a person in your life that will provide spiritual guidance. They will be there for you.

LET US HELP YOU BROADEN YOUR TARGET
this will help you hit your mark

Rita had begun to see her struggles and how they unfolded in her personal story. Three months into therapy, though, her trust still surrounded one person: her therapist. She came to realize some hard truths through sharing and naming her traumatic event. Rita finally said what she had only referred to up to that point as the "r" word, which stood for "rape". While she had sincerely believed she would never begin to trust again, she was finally able to widen that circle with one other person-a lady named Lisa.

Lisa was a few years older than Rita, and was a sharp professional mom. She brought much wisdom and experience to the table. Rita's first team member outside her therapist had finally happened! Her fear began to subside and she was able to fully embrace and accept the "r" word for what it was. She began to realize that she had a major distrust for all men, which was a very emotional discovery for her. She had an "aha" moment through reading the books *Gap and Gain* and *Suffering*. Rita recognized that she did not trust Fred to lead, to parent, or truly know her as a person. She also discovered that although she was surrounded by people nearly all the time, she was lonely.

Her issue with distrust didn't just stop with her husband-she distrusted her children as well. The diaper incident that occurred during their first session was a common scene, but it wasn't until a family meeting that we discovered that June wasn't allowed to care for her siblings.

June was a driven little lady much like her mother. She was a certified babysitter and regularly watched children for other families. Rita admitted during the meeting that she didn't trust June, her husband, or anyone else to change, bathe, or attend to the children's needs. She was petrified that her children would endure anything similar to what she had experienced.

As far as the children were concerned, their behavior was close to perfect. Rita had set up her life to guard against as many life issues as possible. The children were well-rounded kids due to Rita's goals and careful attention, but they had un-written rules (and rightly so). These included:

- No sleep overs
- No group sports
- No public school
- No one cares for their needs except Rita.

Rita was, as we like to say, a momma bear! While these restrictions served their purpose, Rita discovered in therapy that her fear caused her to place herself in the position that brought the family into therapy in the first place: her lack of assistance from Fred.

Rita dealt with fear, but I want to point out that Rita did nothing, and I mean nothing, to cause her traumatic event! Rita had never accepted that the rape even occured. It wasn't until she accepted that the event took place that growth even began. She was learning to forgive.

Fred's acceptance was similar in nature but different in overall execution. Fred was an angry man, with an anger that he neither acknowledged nor took responsibility for. He was angry that he didn't get to play football in high school after the death of his dad. He had aspirations of playing for Notre Dame, and was a self-described Rudy junkie. He knew he was never the biggest guy, but he sure wasn't the smallest either! Fred also had a desire to attend school, and maybe even pursue music as a career.

None of these things came to fruition, however, because Fred had no self-leadership. He was addicted to avoidance. This produced anger, frustration, and a crippling fear of success. He began to discover all the dreams, goals and aspirations he had set aside through writing his story, and he also began to notice his anger toward the two women in his life he was closest to. Fred began to accept that he had allowed others to drive his story.

He was employed at his uncle's car dealership, which was a successful, well-paid job he was really good at. Fred always felt that he really could have been good at anything that he did. He was right, and was beginning to see that while he had not driven his life for a while, with a little help, support, communication of expectations, acceptance, ownership, goal and outcome tracking he could truly bring about change. He also invited his first team member: his uncle. His uncle really believed in him, and knew that Fred really could do whatever he wanted to.

Secretly, his uncle hoped that he would lose Fred as an employee, and not because he wasn't a good worker. On the contrary, his uncle secretly had hopes that he would lose his best employee because he knew Fred's value! Fred's uncle was a visionary and ultimately became Fred's mentor and one of his closest friends.

During Fred's ownership process, he learned that while he did not create nor contribute to the trauma, he did allow others to sculpt his life. This ultimately led to his wife and mother being incredibly lonely as Fred lived most of his life disengaged and on autopilot.

During Rita's ownership process, she learned that while she did not create nor contribute to the trauma, she did sculpt her circle of protection, thus creating the storm of loneliness and self-reliance in her life. Operating in survival mode, Rita had turned on autopilot (the block between the head and the heart).

The key to turning off autopilot is a process referred to as AOGO. This is the key to turning off autopilot due to how this helps us live in the present. Living in the present is the only way to thrive! Think about the movie *Click* with Adam Sandler!

Acceptance, Ownership, Goals and Outcomes:

Acceptance: To acknowledge what has happened to us that we had no control over.

Ownership: What our personal behavior has produced for us in life.

Goals: A measurable and achievable desire.

Outcomes: What the process produced.

Joshua's Acceptance, Ownership, Goals and Outcomes:

Acceptance: *My biological father left me as a child, this was not my fault.*

Ownership: *My actions, be they good or bad, are not controlled by my biological father leaving me.*

Goals: *To never leave my children!*

Outcomes: *I did not leave my boys and was a single parent for years* *prior to my wife Athena coming into our lives.*

Each month we fill out an AOGO chart and adjust as necessary! Accepting what we have not control over, taking ownership of what we can control, developing goals, and tracking outcomes. Don't like the outcome? Repeat, accept what you cannot change, own what you did or did not do, change the goal or repeat a goal and track the outcome! We will rate each team meeting and monthly performance based on the above AOGO.

There are two types of people we discuss in our process. Team Head, the thinkers, and Team Heart the feelers. These two teams tackle action in different ways, allowing thought or feelings to influence their actions. Neither is better than the other, but many times thinkers and feelers frustrate one another. We want you to determine what type of processor you are as well as who the members of your team are. This will help immensely with communication through our team process. What team are you on?

People are either primarily Thinkers or Feelers. We start with our strength, what easily drives us, and work towards our weakness, what is harder for us.

Team Head: The thinkers (thoughts and decisions held in the mind. Who has time for feelings?)

Team Heart: The feelers (there is no reason I placed

us second, except to avoid hurting the thinkers' feelings!) There are many times this is referred to as "gut"! Trust your gut!

One important part of helping your team members learn you better and how to engage with you is to take a personality test. Ahead, you will find a link to the DISC personality test. Once you take the test, write your results on the line provided. This must be done prior to the first team meeting.

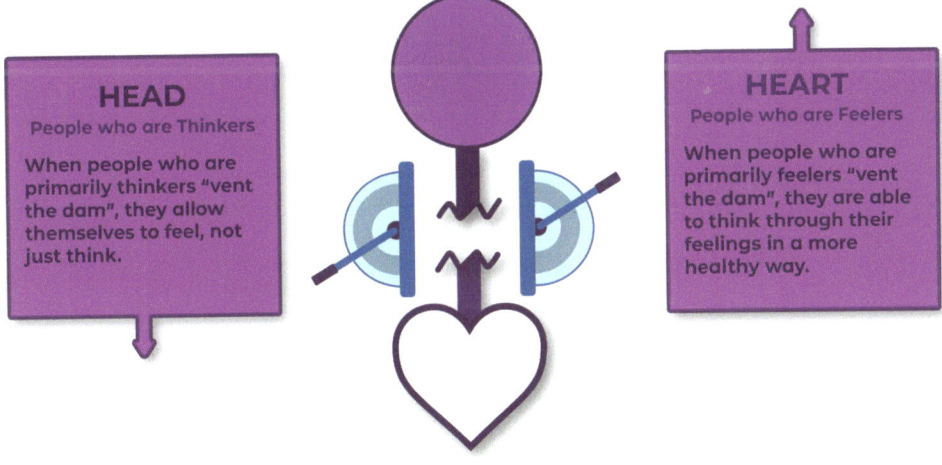

When you have control over your thoughts and feelings, you can then control your emotions. In other words, you can "vent the dam". This means you communicate your thoughts and feelings effectively and in a healthy way. This empowers you, and helps maintain healthy relationships.

HEAD
People who are Thinkers

When people who are primarily thinkers "vent the dam", they allow themselves to feel, not just think.

HEART
People who are Feelers

When people who are primarily feelers "vent the dam", they are able to think through their feelings in a more healthy way.

Visit opendoor406.com/materials and click on "DISC Types Explained" video link.

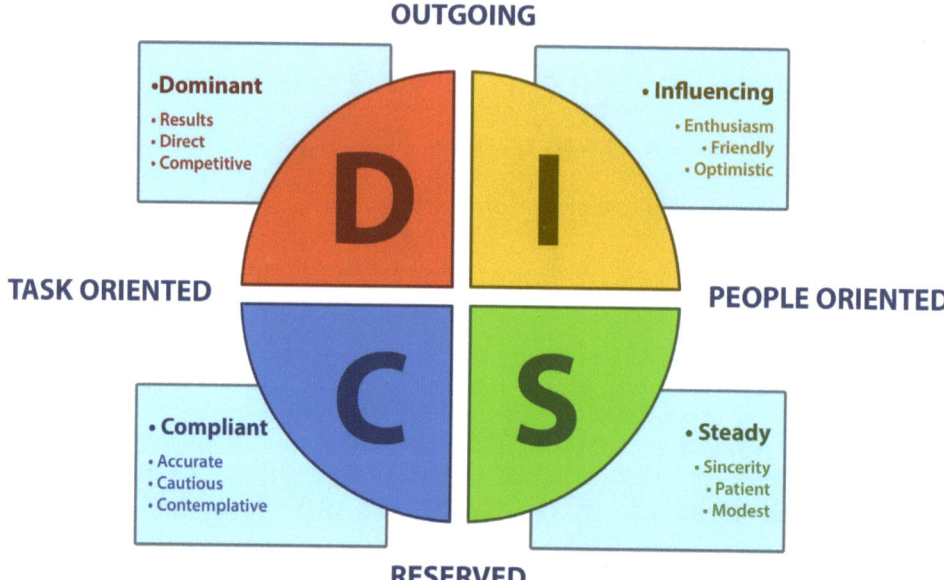

Now that you know your personality type, I want to clarify a few thoughts about personalities:

- Personality is fluid- it has the ability to change
- Personality gives us insight into who we are at our worst.
- Personality results help us know how to weigh out a person's approach.
- There is no right or wrong personality style. We all help one another grow.

Change this:

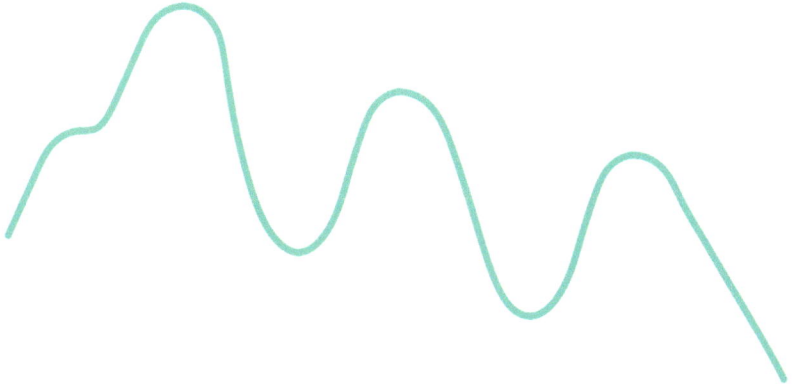

When you are emotionally unstable, your relationships tend to have a lot of highs and lows, and generally go in a downward direction.

To this:

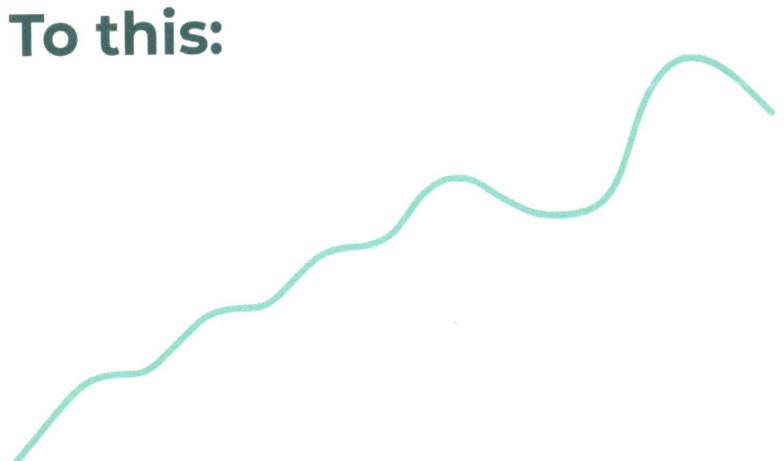

When you gain emotional stability and are given the tools and team to succeed, your relationships are healthier, more steady, and more successful.

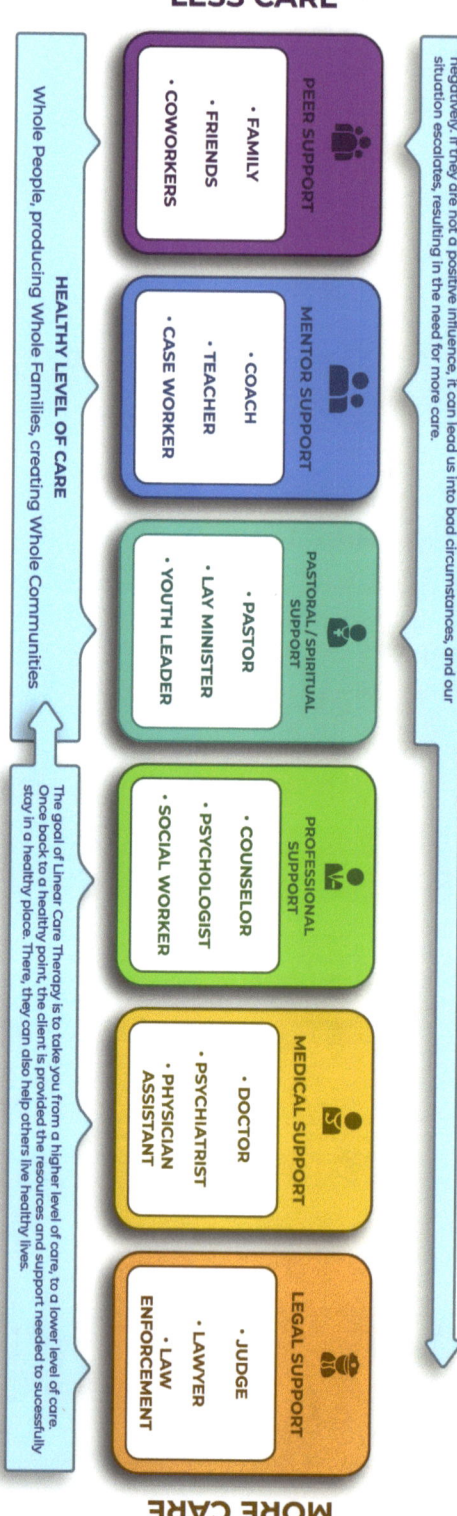

Chapter 9:
Learning to be Zealous!

Now let's look a little more at some guidelines for choosing the right people for your team. You want them to be zealous, meaning they are fervent for your wellbeing. You are absolutely worth it! By "it" I mean place any goal you desire!

By now you also will have read the book *Gap and Gain*, I ask you what is your "Boat Motto"? This is where you set up for yourself a litmus test. Have a statement that can be readily available and asked. Share that statement with your peer and ask it of yourself regularly!

PEER SUPPORT

Peer support: Your primary person! That person who knows you inside and out.

Keyword: vulnerability!

- **Let's chat:** Your peer is a person that is someone you genuinely enjoy spending time with. This relationship is one that is likely the most fluid. Attempt to give back as much as you get with all team members, but make a very

real attempt to know your peer and support him or her in their life as well as allowing them to support you in yours. Be a giver.
- **Grow and truly know:** A person you can grow with and know, and a person who deeply knows you!

Time commitment and expectations: This is the most intense involvement. This person is the person that will go to war with and for you. He or she should be grounded and mature. You want to find a person willing to challenge your thinking- you don't want any "yes" men or women. We must be okay with this person challenging us.

Our peers are the number one indicator of who we will be in our future, whether that's physically, financially, or spiritually. Who you surround yourself with and allow to influence your life will be who you become. If you don't like that thought, or what your future holds, then make the change now. Eventually that choice will be made for you. We all only have so much time.

Time Estimate: 4-6 hours a month
Total time commitment: 72 hours

MENTOR SUPPORT

Mentor: A person who you see as having accomplished something you desire to grow in! A skill, resilience, or an understanding of something that will assist you in becoming the best version of yourself!

- **Let's challenge:** This is a person that you see something in, and a person that you respect. Their goal is to directly challenge you in your thoughts and actions. Allow them the space and ability to say those things that cut! "Wounds from a friend can be trusted" Proverbs 27:6.
- **The thinking:** You're not always right, nor do you have all the answers. I do not care if you are Elon Musk or Plato himself, you have a thing or two to learn. The question is: will you allow these wounds to help you heal?

Time commitment and expectations: Having a mentor is a wonderful thing. If you dig into my family, you will see we are inundated with these folks. Truth be told, we are always learning from someone. This person can either add to your life positively or negatively. Make sure you know what person is adding to your life positive or negative skills. This team member is a person who you see as somewhere you want to be or has a skill you desire to learn.

Time estimation: 2-4 hours per month, depending on chosen area of growth and issues present.

Total time commitment: 48 hours per year

PASTORAL / SPIRITUAL SUPPORT

Pastoral: This is a spiritual guide! A small group leader, a lay minister, or a seasoned person in the faith! This is someone who understands the spiritual you, or at least someone you desire to emulate spiritually!

- **Let's challenge:** This is a person you allow into your life as a spiritual influence. This is also a person that works with you on a spiritual level to break free from bondages that have harmed you. This is commonly referred to as deliverance. We will have much more on this in the version of the book that includes spirituality on a deeper level (goal to release late 2022). At Open Door, we work in depth with Pastor Lee Burrows and Pastor Gloire Ndongala.

- **The theology:** Many times we can find ourselves with wounds from a particular church congregation. There are no perfect churches, only a perfect Savior, Jesus. Allow yourself to evaluate what it is you think you know or don't. Allow your team the ability to all discuss these things. Determine if you have religion or relationship.

- **The church wounds (if present):** Open up! Don't leave anything hidden! Expose your story!

Time commitment and expectations: This varies depending on issues surrounding your spiritual health. As previously stated, this is a pivotal piece of every single person. We encourage you to be involved in a church and a small group. If you don't have one, we have several pastors and groups that work closely with us in this process. We ask you to find a spiritually mature person who can challenge your thoughts and ideas surrounding religion/spirituality.

Time estimation: 1-3 hours per month depending on spiritual issues present.

Total time commitment: 24 hours per year

PROFESSIONAL SUPPORT

Professional: This is the counselor, dietitian, or professional guide to beginning to understand you and who you desire to become! In essence, this is the "mapmaker"!

- **Let's challenge:** This role is reserved for a trained specialist in mental health. We like to refer to it as "kicking it up". This is not to say that a professional is more important than other team members, but is to say that training in dealing with a mental or physical issue is valuable.

- **The behaviors:** Many times we find ourselves with

actions, thoughts, feelings that we neither invite or have control over. ATP is designed to get these out and bring healing to your mind and heart.

Time Commitment and expectations: You need a therapist who will walk with you and have clear-cut, well-defined and well-explained processes and tactics to help you move toward your established goals. As you can see, the Anchored Process is clearly defined and upfront. A therapist should always be able to answer the question about his or her theoretical orientation. As with all professionals and all processes, you get out what you put into it.

I hope that this book and our Anchored therapy model shows our commitment to offering you the best care possible. We are the first line of defense in the professional realm. This is evident in that we work to help change behavior while you still have options. Please do not wait until you have medical or legal trauma to make changes in your life!

Time estimation: 4-6 hours per month depending on mental health issues present.

Total time commitment: Est. 53 hours per year

MEDICAL SUPPORT

Medical: How many of us have been faithful in the prevention of health struggles? If your physical health suffers, you are focused on just that! We treat the physical as well as mental and spiritual, but without a body you are not getting far! Let us help you care for your physical body!

- **Let's challenge:** We often neglect our physical health, and ATP addresses this head on! You must get checked out and engage with or find a PCM. We should not treat the psychological without understanding where a person is physically. Mind, body, spirit cannot be separated, and all must be addressed.
- **The body:** So many of us are unhealthy but have desires of physically feeling better. Addressing physical health is essential for wholeness.

Time commitment and expectations: This varies depending on medical issues present and care you've received in the past. We do require a physical, current blood work, and a health panel. We would be amiss to treat the psychological without first ruling out physical issues and determining health. We partner with Open Door Medical Clinic (Dr. Mel Parmley and Jamie Barns) for medical integration in house. We will gladly work with any physician collaboratively! Mental and physical issues left untreated lead to medical failure of some system or systems. Your body can only survive under a load of stress for so long.

Time estimation: 1-3 hours per month depending on physical issues present.

Total time commitment: 24 hours per year

LEGAL SUPPORT

Legal: When we have legal trouble, we are having care imposed upon us! This is still care. Do not neglect yourself or those you love to the point where people stop you legally. If you find yourself with legal issues, we will incorporate these supporters in your care as to get us all on the same page! Stay in the fight!

- **Aligning the system and the person:** If you have involvement with the law, we want their input on the team. If you do not have involvement from the law, let's get this life stuff under control so no one has to step in and take freedom away as a means to help you survive.

Time commitment and expectations: Be it law enforcement, judges, or attorneys, remember that these people are there to help you. This is difficult, and no one desires to find themselves having a system intercede because of your behavior. However, know that all mental health issues lead here, whether they're addiction or just pure mental issues. Left untreated, we end up with some type of legal involvement.

Time estimation: 1-3 hours per month depending on legal issues present.

Total time commitment: 24 hours per year

In the following video, we define expectations and roles and responsibilities that address many of our most commonly asked questions. Happy hunting!

Visit opendoor406.com/materials and click on "How to Master Recruiting" video link.

Fred and Rita's dream team!

Fred and Rita began treatment with little to no expectations, similar to many other couples or individuals who have come into the clinic throughout the years. At this point in their care, they had recruited their entire team. Let's take a look at who they head-hunted and give a little background to help you understand their personal why's!

Rita

Peer: *Lisa, a pro mom who was always seeking Rita out and seeing how she was prior to coming to the clinic.*

Mentor: *Samantha, a local restaurant owner, who Rita loved to chat with about how to run a company. Samantha had a regular patronage and Rita loved how open and trusting Sam appeared to those she knew.*

Spiritual: *A couple named Rick and Rhen who led a small group at their church. This couple pursued Fred and Rita for about a year before they attended their first small group, which happened after they started therapy.*

Professional: *Anchored Therapist*

Medical: *A local ND who worked with women's health issues. Rita had gone years without any medical care. While she herself was an NP who regularly addressed women's issues, Rita opened up that she had neglected any annual visits. In the end, she found a few issues that she had to medically address.*

Legal: *The family was blessed to not have legal issues when in our process; however, if any more time had progressed, they most likely would have. Both Fred and Rita had admitted to speaking with attorneys but not pursuing anything legally.*

Fred

Peer: *Uncle Mark, a man and a boss who truly believed in Fred.*

Mentor: *Steve, a local pharmacist from church who had sought out a second career after leaving sales at his uncle's business. Steve, a man who loved Fred from the time he worked at the dealership, died laughing every time he would talk about the pay cut he took to pursue his dream of being a pharmacist. He was always told he wasn't good enough, and Steve loved to help people prove others wrong (with the right motives).*

Spiritual: *A couple who led a small group at their church. Rick and Rhen. This was a couple who pursued Fred and Rita for about a year before they attended their first small group, which happened after starting therapy.*

Professional: *Anchored therapist*

Medical: *Fred sought out medical care from his wife, Rita! This was comical and I loved how Rita played multiple roles on the team. She was thorough, and we had great updates without question as Rita dove in loving to share her knowledge. Truth be told, we loved her to share it!*

Legal: *The family was blessed to not have legal issues when in our process, however if any more time had progressed, they would have. Both Fred and Rita had admitted to speaking with attorneys but not pursuing anything legally.*

Our first team meeting was a trip. We had all the adults and the children present! June, John, and Jude stole the show. They would later describe in innocence how they just loved that their parents invited people in to help. In the past, Rita hadn't allowed people to get close to them. This was to protect her family, but it nearly cost her everything.

Fred, not being engaged or present, brought little to no understanding of who or what a dad should be to his children. Later in the meetings, Fred openly admitted that being present physically but absent in every other way was probably more confusing than when he himself lost his father in the accident.

The team thrived and change began to take hold! This was the beginning of honesty and openness among the family. You can read their full story in the *Anchored* novel.

Your FIRST Team

We've talked extensively about the team we intended to help you create during this process. Many of you at this point will have already created your extended team. This section here is about your first team, your family of origin, your immediate family, your spouse, and your children.

Honestly, there are issues in every family. We have these issues permeating all sorts of media, and stories. From biblical times to the sitcoms of the 90's to the so called social media of today-the world has a view of family that we embrace, and at times, sometimes need to chase away!

There is a therapeutic joke that goes, "If it is not one thing, it's your mother"! Looking at any infant at birth, I can promise you that it could not be further from the truth.

So many of our wounds can be traced right back to our families. This is true for many reasons. Also, this is not true for many other reasons! FAMILY- Fear-Filled, Angry, Maladapted, Illogical, Loving, Yours. You don't get to choose them, and they walk with you sometimes and desert you at other times. You work these issues out during your therapy processing with your team.

Identify your family of origin. Take a few moments and share an example of a circumstance similar to Joshua's. Make this AOGO about your immediate family or family of origin (i.e. mom, dad, siblings, grandparents, aunts and uncles).

Acceptance:

Ownership:

Goals:

Outcome:

All relationships start out in a relational neutral then quickly enter a honeymoon phase. One of the primary premises of the ATP is that there are only so many rejections a person can endure until emotional separation/divorce. A rejection for this purpose is anytime a person has reached out for attention but been denied.

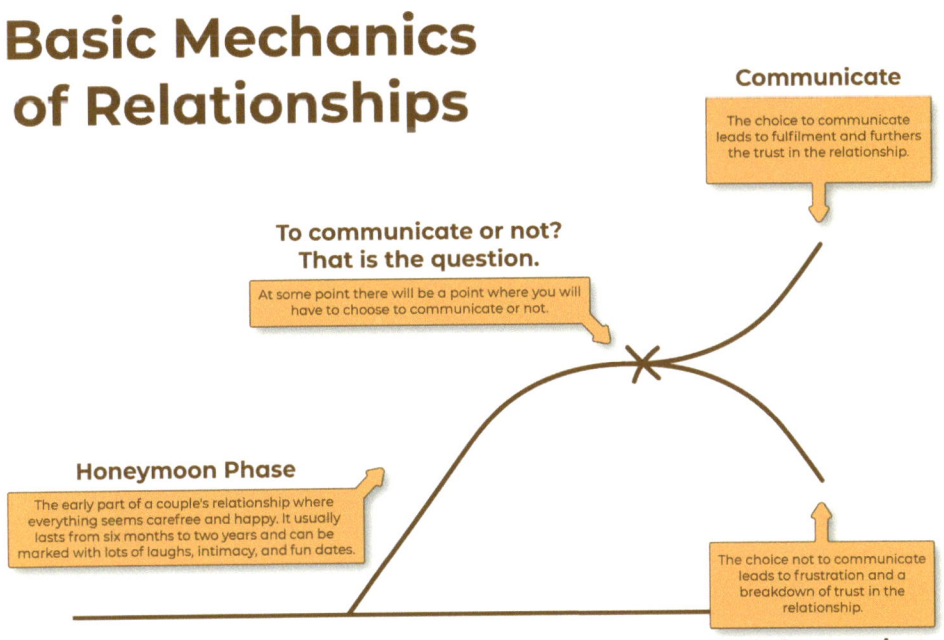

Chapter 10:
What is or Was Doesn't Define the Future!

As we've previously discussed, throwing a fit doesn't get you to where you want to go. What's interesting is that the definition of "fit" is to be of a suitable quality, standard, or type to meet the required purpose. It also refers to being in good health.

I find words to be so powerful. We say so often we are throwing a fit, when in fact something is out of whack (think: a misbehaving toddler in the grocery aisle). I say we take back the term "fit" and make it work for us and not against us! So let's throw a fit together!

Relationship conceptions: FIT: Focused, Intentional, Thoughtful.

Let's reframe a "fit" as being more than just someone being a brat, but rather being a key indicator that something is off:

- A way to address emotions through tough times in care!
- Always call a team member when you are struggling,

Here is a spot for team members to sign in agreement to being contacted and being available.

1.

2.

3.

4.

5.

6.

While you are waiting for a call back, do the exercise below! This can be done anytime stress occurs!

- **Taking back control exercise:** Read through all instructions prior to starting.
  - Find a seat and get comfortable in your chair.
  - Ensure you are safe.
  - You will need a candle and a lighter for this video. Please be responsible with the fire.
  - Visit opendoor406.com/materials and click on "Breathing Exercise" video link. Pull up the video so you are ready to play it when the time comes.
  - Ground your feet firmly. Get yourself ready for a video exercise.
  - Play the video.
- **Thinking back exercise:** Recall a fond memory.
  - Meeting your spouse
  - First time holding your child

- When you first saw your mom or dad after a bad experience
- Hugging your best friend after a summer vacation
- First seeing your first love
- Write down your thoughts/feelings:

Describe the situation:

What is your primary emotion?

How long did that feeling stay until it was replaced?

What was the feeling/situation that replaced it?

I challenge you to think/feel through a relationship and see if there was not a time of neutrality or honeymoon phases.

Two things are missing from the current relationships we're in. These tools are so important that we include them in this workbook. These are explored in depth in therapy, but we need them now!

Delivery: How you say it verbally or nonverbally is the key to being heard.

Intentionality: Most of us recall a honeymoon phase of a relationship somewhere in our history. These phases always have a few things in common.

- We look at FIT for the answer or proverbial key to unlocking the honeymoon phase again!
    - **Focused:** Get rid of all distractions (turn off the game, put down the phone, pull over the car).
    - **Intentional:** Before you had the relationship with the person you are fighting with many times you placed their thoughts, feelings, hopes, aspirations above your own. You listened to them. Do it again! You got the relationship by doing that, now give it the TLC it deserves and do it again.
    - **Thoughtful:** Stop half way (nicest way to say this) engaging in relationships. You have thoughts of your loved one. When these come, ACT on them right then and right there.
- Look at the last fit your loved one threw and ask yourself if you were FIT for a relationship that day.
    - They were seeking a response, throwing a fit, fighting a fit with ATP FIT works!

Start with these tools mentioned above, and we will have forms linked ahead to give you access to tracking outcomes! We require a fully filled out workbook for graduation. This is non-negotiable. To graduate the program and become a lifelong A-Team member you must have fully completed Anchored.

Love you all! Know that you're worth the time you invest in yourself and that you *will* be the next success!

Chapter 11:
Kintsugi ("Joining with Gold")

Kintsugi is a process that takes something that is broken, and by all means worthless, and reconstructs it into a beautiful work of art. My wife and I love pottery, and have had friends in the past who have thrown pottery.

Throwing pottery is a method of forming pottery vessels on a potter's wheel. This method of pot formation was used by ancient Greek potters when they made their vases and is still used today. Pottery is not only useful, it is often beautiful, truly a work of art, literally at the hands of an artisan.

I shared with you that I'm a man of faith, and I hope that if you've made it to this point in the book, the spiritual aspects of the book have not been offensive. At best, I hope that you've possibly been able to work through past hurts and offenses even with the church. The Bible says that God is the potter, and we are the clay. Whether you are or are not a Christian, I hope you can see the beauty in that statement. Someone took the care to form you. The Bible also says He formed us all for different purposes. You are a pot, friends. What you pour in will fill you up, good or bad.

In the end, we are all broken. As broken pots, we can often feel useless and can even be frustrating or harmful for those around us. The Anchored Process and the A-Team are here to be the "gold" that puts you back together, making you a more valuable and useful piece of art. The Bible also describes you as a masterpiece. I hold on to some hope that you know you are a masterpiece by now as well or at least are on the journey of embracing yourself as such. Always remember kintsugi rejoins the pottery after it has been broken. It is your very brokenness that makes you valuable.

This whole process has been preparing you for the journey ahead! The skills you are learning or have learned here are lessons that can benefit us all. Ever heard the old saying, "Wash, Rinse, Repeat"? Well, if you find yourself slipping back into that back seat, then "wash, rinse, repeat"-go back to the beginning of this book and start the process over. Refinement is so often a process that takes time, but you and your loved ones are worth the time you invest! Things in your life did not get thrown out of whack overnight, and they are nearly never fixed overnight.

Again, know that just like in the kintsugi process pottery is joined with gold, your team is the "gold" that joins you! Gold is incredibly heavy, and we all know one of the most valuable items on the planet. Your team is worth its weight in gold. Never forget that, and if you do, get back to your motto and your goals and wash, rinse, and repeat. "Innovation is Mastery" (Unknown) only once you master you can you innovate the world around you! Put that pot back together and the sky's the limits to what you can do with it!

Never fear getting back to the basics! These things are not complicated. They may be difficult, but not complicated. Don't fall into the trap of complicating something that doesn't need to be. Stay in the fight (SITF) and never forget you are worth fighting for!

References

1. *Segway - Definition, Meaning & Synonyms.* (n.d.). Vocabulary.com. Retrieved May 20, 2022, from https://www.vocabulary.com/dictionary/Segway

2. *Segue Definition & Meaning.* (n.d.). Merriam-Webster. Retrieved May 20, 2022, from https://www.merriam-webster.com/dictionary/segue

3. *Chaos Definition & Meaning.* (2022, May 10). Merriam-Webster. Retrieved May 20, 2022, from https://www.merriam-webster.com/dictionary/chaos

4. *DENIAL | definition in the Cambridge English Dictionary.* (n.d.). Cambridge Dictionary. Retrieved May 20, 2022, from https://dictionary.cambridge.org/us/dictionary/english/denial

5. *Control Definition & Meaning.* (n.d.). Merriam-Webster. Retrieved May 20, 2022, from https://www.merriam-webster.com/dictionary/control

6. *Influence Definition & Meaning.* (2022, May 11). Merriam-Webster. Retrieved May 20, 2022, from https://www.merriam-webster.com/dictionary/influence

7. *Expectation - Definition, Meaning & Synonyms.* (n.d.). Vocabulary.com. Retrieved May 20, 2022, from https://www.vocabulary.com/dictionary/expectation

Therapy Session Forms

Quarter 1: REAL Notes

Session:

Reality: it is what it is

Encouragement: the truth is, it doesn't have to play on repeat

Acceptance: we accept the garbage as something we can't change

Leadership: we take out the garbage we can change

Story Update:

Team Meeting Evaluation (circle one)

1 2 3 4 5 6 7 8 9 10
very negative   very positive

Why?

COPYWRITE 2022 JOSHUA HOLLOWAY

Quarter 1: REAL Notes

Session:

Reality: it is what it is

Encouragement: the truth is, it doesn't have to play on repeat

Acceptance: we accept the garbage as something we can't change

Leadership: we take out the garbage we can change

Story Update:

Team Meeting Evaluation (circle one)

1   2   3   4   5   6   7   8   9   10

very negative   very positive

Why?

COPYWRITE 2022 JOSHUA HOLLOWAY

Quarter 1: REAL Notes

Session:

Reality: it is what it is

Encouragement: the truth is, it doesn't have to play on repeat

Acceptance: we accept the garbage as something we can't change

Leadership: we take out the garbage we can change

Story Update:

Team Meeting Evaluation (circle one)

1   2   3   4   5   6   7   8   9   10

very negative   very positive

Why?

COPYWRITE 2022 JOSHUA HOLLOWAY

Quarter 1: REAL Notes

Session:

Reality: it is what it is

Encouragement: the truth is, it doesn't have to play on repeat

Acceptance: we accept the garbage as something we can't change

Leadership: we take out the garbage we can change

Story Update:

Team Meeting Evaluation (circle one)

1   2   3   4   5   6   7   8   9   10

very negative   very positive

Why?

Quarter 1: REAL Notes

Session:

Reality: it is what it is

Encouragement: the truth is, it doesn't have to play on repeat

Acceptance: we accept the garbage as something we can't change

Leadership: we take out the garbage we can change

Story Update:

Team Meeting Evaluation (circle one)

1   2   3   4   5   6   7   8   9   10

very negative   very positive

Why?

COPYWRITE 2022 JOSHUA HOLLOWAY

Quarter 1: REAL Notes

Session:

Reality: it is what it is

Encouragement: the truth is, it doesn't have to play on repeat

Acceptance: we accept the garbage as something we can't change

Leadership: we take out the garbage we can change

Story Update:

Team Meeting Evaluation (circle one)

1   2   3   4   5   6   7   8   9   10

very negative   very positive

Why?

COPYWRITE 2022 JOSHUA HOLLOWAY

Quarter 1: REAL Notes

Session:

Reality: it is what it is

Encouragement: the truth is, it doesn't have to play on repeat

Acceptance: we accept the garbage as something we can't change

Leadership: we take out the garbage we can change

Story Update:

Team Meeting Evaluation (circle one)

1　　2　　3　　4　　5　　6　　7　　8　　9　　10

very negative　　　　　　　　　　　　　　　　very positive

Why?

COPYWRITE 2022 JOSHUA HOLLOWAY

Quarter 1: REAL Notes

Session:

Reality: it is what it is

Encouragement: the truth is, it doesn't have to play on repeat

Acceptance: we accept the garbage as something we can't change

Leadership: we take out the garbage we can change

Story Update:

Team Meeting Evaluation (circle one)

1   2   3   4   5   6   7   8   9   10
very   very
negative   positive

Why?

COPYWRITE 2022 JOSHUA HOLLOWAY

Quarter 1: REAL Notes

Session:

Reality: it is what it is

Encouragement: the truth is, it doesn't have to play on repeat

Acceptance: we accept the garbage as something we can't change

Leadership: we take out the garbage we can change

Story Update:

Team Meeting Evaluation (circle one)

1   2   3   4   5   6   7   8   9   10

very negative   very positive

Why?

COPYWRITE 2022 JOSHUA HOLLOWAY

Quarter 1: REAL Notes

Session:

Reality: it is what it is

Encouragement: the truth is, it doesn't have to play on repeat

Acceptance: we accept the garbage as something we can't change

Leadership: we take out the garbage we can change

Story Update:

Team Meeting Evaluation (circle one)

1   2   3   4   5   6   7   8   9   10

very negative   very positive

Why?

COPYWRITE 2022 JOSHUA HOLLOWAY

Quarter 1: REAL Notes

Session:

Reality: it is what it is

Encouragement: the truth is, it doesn't have to play on repeat

Acceptance: we accept the garbage as something we can't change

Leadership: we take out the garbage we can change

Story Update:

Team Meeting Evaluation (circle one)

1 2 3 4 5 6 7 8 9 10

very negative   very positive

Why?

COPYWRITE 2022 JOSHUA HOLLOWAY

Quarter 1: REAL Notes

Session:

Reality: it is what it is

Encouragement: the truth is, it doesn't have to play on repeat

Acceptance: we accept the garbage as something we can't change

Leadership: we take out the garbage we can change

Story Update:

Team Meeting Evaluation (circle one)

1   2   3   4   5   6   7   8   9   10

very negative   very positive

Why?

COPYWRITE 2022 JOSHUA HOLLOWAY

Quarter 2: REAL Notes

Session:

Reality: it is what it is

Encouragement: the truth is, it doesn't have to play on repeat

Acceptance: we accept the garbage as something we can't change

Leadership: we take out the garbage we can change

Story Update:

Team Meeting Evaluation (circle one)

1   2   3   4   5   6   7   8   9   10
very   very
negative   positive

Why?

COPYWRITE 2022 JOSHUA HOLLOWAY

Quarter 2: REAL Notes

Session:

Reality: it is what it is

Encouragement: the truth is, it doesn't have to play on repeat

Acceptance: we accept the garbage as something we can't change

Leadership: we take out the garbage we can change

Story Update:

Team Meeting Evaluation (circle one)

1   2   3   4   5   6   7   8   9   10

very negative   very positive

Why?

Quarter 2: REAL Notes

Session:

Reality: it is what it is

Encouragement: the truth is, it doesn't have to play on repeat

Acceptance: we accept the garbage as something we can't change

Leadership: we take out the garbage we can change

Story Update:

Team Meeting Evaluation (circle one)

1　　2　　3　　4　　5　　6　　7　　8　　9　　10
very　　　　　　　　　　　　　　　　　　　　very
negative　　　　　　　　　　　　　　　　　positive

Why?

COPYWRITE 2022 JOSHUA HOLLOWAY

Quarter 2: REAL Notes

Session:

Reality: it is what it is

Encouragement: the truth is, it doesn't have to play on repeat

Acceptance: we accept the garbage as something we can't change

Leadership: we take out the garbage we can change

Story Update:

Team Meeting Evaluation (circle one)

1   2   3   4   5   6   7   8   9   10
very negative   very positive

Why?

COPYWRITE 2022 JOSHUA HOLLOWAY

Quarter 2: REAL Notes

Session:

Reality: it is what it is

Encouragement: the truth is, it doesn't have to play on repeat

Acceptance: we accept the garbage as something we can't change

Leadership: we take out the garbage we can change

Story Update:

Team Meeting Evaluation (circle one)

1   2   3   4   5   6   7   8   9   10
very negative   very positive

Why?

COPYWRITE 2022 JOSHUA HOLLOWAY

Quarter 2: REAL Notes

Session:

Reality: it is what it is

Encouragement: the truth is, it doesn't have to play on repeat

Acceptance: we accept the garbage as something we can't change

Leadership: we take out the garbage we can change

Story Update:

Team Meeting Evaluation (circle one)

1   2   3   4   5   6   7   8   9   10
very   very
negative   positive

Why?

COPYWRITE 2022 JOSHUA HOLLOWAY

Quarter 2: REAL Notes

Session:

Reality: it is what it is

Encouragement: the truth is, it doesn't have to play on repeat

Acceptance: we accept the garbage as something we can't change

Leadership: we take out the garbage we can change

Story Update:

Team Meeting Evaluation (circle one)

1   2   3   4   5   6   7   8   9   10

very negative   very positive

Why?

Quarter 2: REAL Notes

Session:

Reality: it is what it is

Encouragement: the truth is, it doesn't have to play on repeat

Acceptance: we accept the garbage as something we can't change

Leadership: we take out the garbage we can change

Story Update:

Team Meeting Evaluation (circle one)

1   2   3   4   5   6   7   8   9   10
very   very
negative   positive

Why?

COPYWRITE 2022 JOSHUA HOLLOWAY

Quarter 2: REAL Notes

Session:

Reality: it is what it is

Encouragement: the truth is, it doesn't have to play on repeat

Acceptance: we accept the garbage as something we can't change

Leadership: we take out the garbage we can change

Story Update:

Team Meeting Evaluation (circle one)

1   2   3   4   5   6   7   8   9   10

very negative   very positive

Why?

COPYWRITE 2022 JOSHUA HOLLOWAY

Quarter 2: REAL Notes

Session:

Reality: it is what it is

Encouragement: the truth is, it doesn't have to play on repeat

Acceptance: we accept the garbage as something we can't change

Leadership: we take out the garbage we can change

Story Update:

Team Meeting Evaluation (circle one)

1   2   3   4   5   6   7   8   9   10
very   very
negative   positive

Why?

COPYWRITE 2022 JOSHUA HOLLOWAY

Quarter 2: REAL Notes

Session:

Reality: it is what it is

Encouragement: the truth is, it doesn't have to play on repeat

Acceptance: we accept the garbage as something we can't change

Leadership: we take out the garbage we can change

Story Update:

Team Meeting Evaluation (circle one)

1   2   3   4   5   6   7   8   9   10

very negative   very positive

Why?

Quarter 2: REAL Notes

Session:

Reality: it is what it is

Encouragement: the truth is, it doesn't have to play on repeat

Acceptance: we accept the garbage as something we can't change

Leadership: we take out the garbage we can change

Story Update:

Team Meeting Evaluation (circle one)
1 2 3 4 5 6 7 8 9 10
very   very
negative   positive

Comfort with every other week (circle one)
1 2 3 4 5 6 7 8 9 10
very   very
negative   positive

Why?

COPYWRITE 2022 JOSHUA HOLLOWAY

Quarter 3: REAL Notes

Session:

Reality: it is what it is

Encouragement: the truth is, it doesn't have to play on repeat

Acceptance: we accept the garbage as something we can't change

Leadership: we take out the garbage we can change

Story Update:

Team Meeting Evaluation (circle one)

1   2   3   4   5   6   7   8   9   10

very negative   very positive

Why?

Quarter 3: REAL Notes

Session:

Reality: it is what it is

Encouragement: the truth is, it doesn't have to play on repeat

Acceptance: we accept the garbage as something we can't change

Leadership: we take out the garbage we can change

Story Update:

Team Meeting Evaluation (circle one)

1　　2　　3　　4　　5　　6　　7　　8　　9　　10
very　　　　　　　　　　　　　　　　　　　　very
negative　　　　　　　　　　　　　　　　　　positive

Why?

COPYWRITE 2022 JOSHUA HOLLOWAY

Quarter 3: REAL Notes

Session:

Reality: it is what it is

Encouragement: the truth is, it doesn't have to play on repeat

Acceptance: we accept the garbage as something we can't change

Leadership: we take out the garbage we can change

Story Update:

Team Meeting Evaluation (circle one)

1   2   3   4   5   6   7   8   9   10
very   very
negative   positive

Why?

COPYWRITE 2022 JOSHUA HOLLOWAY

Quarter 3: REAL Notes

Session:

Reality: it is what it is

Encouragement: the truth is, it doesn't have to play on repeat

Acceptance: we accept the garbage as something we can't change

Leadership: we take out the garbage we can change

Story Update:

Team Meeting Evaluation (circle one)

1 2 3 4 5 6 7 8 9 10
very negative   very positive

Why?

COPYWRITE 2022 JOSHUA HOLLOWAY

Quarter 3: REAL Notes

Session:

Reality: it is what it is

Encouragement: the truth is, it doesn't have to play on repeat

Acceptance: we accept the garbage as something we can't change

Leadership: we take out the garbage we can change

Story Update:

Team Meeting Evaluation (circle one)

1   2   3   4   5   6   7   8   9   10
very   very
negative   positive

Why?

COPYWRITE 2022 JOSHUA HOLLOWAY

Quarter 3: REAL Notes

Session:

Reality: it is what it is

Encouragement: the truth is, it doesn't have to play on repeat

Acceptance: we accept the garbage as something we can't change

Leadership: we take out the garbage we can change

Story Update:

Team Meeting Evaluation (circle one)
1 2 3 4 5 6 7 8 9 10
very   very
negative   positive

Comfort with once monthly (circle one)
1 2 3 4 5 6 7 8 9 10
very   very
negative   positive

Why?

COPYWRITE 2022 JOSHUA HOLLOWAY

Quarter 4: REAL Notes

Session:

Reality: it is what it is

Encouragement: the truth is, it doesn't have to play on repeat

Acceptance: we accept the garbage as something we can't change

Leadership: we take out the garbage we can change

Story Update:

Team Meeting Evaluation (circle one)

1   2   3   4   5   6   7   8   9   10
very negative   very positive

Why?

Quarter 4: REAL Notes

Session:

Reality: it is what it is

Encouragement: the truth is, it doesn't have to play on repeat

Acceptance: we accept the garbage as something we can't change

Leadership: we take out the garbage we can change

Story Update:

Team Meeting Evaluation (circle one)

1   2   3   4   5   6   7   8   9   10
very   very
negative   positive

Why?

COPYWRITE 2022 JOSHUA HOLLOWAY

Quarter 4: REAL Notes

Session:

Reality: it is what it is

Encouragement: the truth is, it doesn't have to play on repeat

Acceptance: we accept the garbage as something we can't change

Leadership: we take out the garbage we can change

Story Update:

Team Meeting Evaluation (circle one)

1   2   3   4   5   6   7   8   9   10
very   very
negative   positive

Why?

COPYWRITE 2022 JOSHUA HOLLOWAY

Quarter 4: REAL Notes

Session:

Reality: it is what it is

Encouragement: the truth is, it doesn't have to play on repeat

Acceptance: we accept the garbage as something we can't change

Leadership: we take out the garbage we can change

Story Update:

Team Meeting Evaluation (circle one)

1   2   3   4   5   6   7   8   9   10

very negative   very positive

Why?

COPYWRITE 2022 JOSHUA HOLLOWAY

Graduation weekend planning! We are so proud of you! Invite a team member of your choice for the retreat and ceremony!

Continuing therapy! Therapy never ends, but professional therapy does. We love you and always know if you ever need us we are here!

Go kick life's butt!

BookIt! Forms

Therapy BookIt!

Which book did you read?
- [ ] Gap and Gain
- [ ] Extreme Ownership
- [ ] Suffering
- [ ] The Goal
- [ ] Atomic Habits
- [ ] Leadership Pain
- [ ] _____
- [ ] _____
- [ ] _____
- [ ] _____
- [ ] _____
- [ ] _____

Application: what was interesting?

What did you do with the information? (Action required)

What was your AHA moment? (Didn't get one? Re-read it or give an explination why)

Book Specific Homework written out:

Journal Prompts

Exercises

What hope did you find?

Do you recommend this book to someone else? (circle one)

1   2   3   4   5   6   7   8   9   10
not at all   absolutely

Why?

Any suggestions for the therapy team?

COPYWRITE 2022 JOSHUA HOLLOWAY

Therapy BookIt!

Which book did you read?
- [ ] Gap and Gain
- [ ] Extreme Ownership
- [ ] Suffering
- [ ] The Goal
- [ ] Atomic Habits
- [ ] Leadership Pain
- [ ] _____
- [ ] _____
- [ ] _____
- [ ] _____
- [ ] _____
- [ ] _____

Application: what was interesting?

What did you do with the information? (Action required)

What was your AHA moment? (Didn't get one? Re-read it or give an explination why)

Book Specific Homework written out:

Journal Prompts

Exercises

What hope did you find?

Do you recommend this book to someone else? (circle one)

1   2   3   4   5   6   7   8   9   10
not at all   absolutely

Why?

Any suggestions for the therapy team?

COPYWRITE 2022 JOSHUA HOLLOWAY

Therapy BookIt!

Which book did you read?
- [ ] Gap and Gain
- [ ] Extreme Ownership
- [ ] Suffering
- [ ] The Goal
- [ ] Atomic Habits
- [ ] Leadership Pain
- [ ] _____
- [ ] _____
- [ ] _____
- [ ] _____
- [ ] _____
- [ ] _____

Application: what was interesting?

What did you do with the information? (Action required)

What was your AHA moment? (Didn't get one? Re-read it or give an explination why)

Book Specific Homework written out:

Journal Prompts _____

Exercises _____

What hope did you find?

Do you recommend this book to someone else? (circle one)

1   2   3   4   5   6   7   8   9   10

not at all   absolutely

Why?

Any suggestions for the therapy team?

COPYWRITE 2022 JOSHUA HOLLOWAY

Therapy BookIt!

Which book did you read?

- [ ] Gap and Gain
- [ ] Extreme Ownership
- [ ] Suffering
- [ ] The Goal
- [ ] Atomic Habits
- [ ] Leadership Pain
- [ ] _____
- [ ] _____
- [ ] _____
- [ ] _____
- [ ] _____
- [ ] _____

Application: what was interesting?

What did you do with the information? (Action required)

What was your AHA moment? (Didn't get one? Re-read it or give an explination why)

Book Specific Homework written out:

Journal Prompts

Exercises

What hope did you find?

Do you recommend this book to someone else? (circle one)

1   2   3   4   5   6   7   8   9   10
not at all   absolutely

Why?

Any suggestions for the therapy team?

COPYWRITE 2022 JOSHUA HOLLOWAY

Therapy BookIt!

Which book did you read?
- [ ] Gap and Gain
- [ ] Extreme Ownership
- [ ] Suffering
- [ ] The Goal
- [ ] Atomic Habits
- [ ] Leadership Pain
- [ ] _____
- [ ] _____
- [ ] _____
- [ ] _____
- [ ] _____
- [ ] _____

Application: what was interesting?

What did you do with the information? (Action required)

What was your AHA moment? (Didn't get one? Re-read it or give an explination why)

Book Specific Homework written out:

Journal Prompts

Exercises

What hope did you find?

Do you recommend this book to someone else? (circle one)

1   2   3   4   5   6   7   8   9   10
not at all   absolutely

Why?

Any suggestions for the therapy team?

COPYWRITE 2022 JOSHUA HOLLOWAY

Therapy BookIt!

Which book did you read?
- [ ] Gap and Gain
- [ ] Extreme Ownership
- [ ] Suffering
- [ ] The Goal
- [ ] Atomic Habits
- [ ] Leadership Pain
- [ ] _____
- [ ] _____
- [ ] _____
- [ ] _____
- [ ] _____
- [ ] _____

Application: what was interesting?

What did you do with the information? (Action required)

What was your AHA moment? (Didn't get one? Re-read it or give an explination why)

Book Specific Homework written out:

Journal Prompts

Exercises

What hope did you find?

Do you recommend this book to someone else? (circle one)

1   2   3   4   5   6   7   8   9   10

not at all   absolutely

Why?

Any suggestions for the therapy team?

COPYWRITE 2022 JOSHUA HOLLOWAY

Therapy BookIt!

Which book did you read?
- [ ] Gap and Gain
- [ ] Extreme Ownership
- [ ] Suffering
- [ ] The Goal
- [ ] Atomic Habits
- [ ] Leadership Pain
- [ ] _____
- [ ] _____
- [ ] _____
- [ ] _____
- [ ] _____
- [ ] _____

Application: what was interesting?

What did you do with the information? (Action required)

What was your AHA moment? (Didn't get one? Re-read it or give an explination why)

Book Specific Homework written out:

Journal Prompts

Exercises

What hope did you find?

Do you recommend this book to someone else? (circle one)

1　2　3　4　5　6　7　8　9　10
not at all　　　　　　　　　　　　　absolutely

Why?

Any suggestions for the therapy team?

COPYWRITE 2022 JOSHUA HOLLOWAY

Therapy BookIt!

Which book did you read?
- ☐ Gap and Gain
- ☐ Extreme Ownership
- ☐ Suffering
- ☐ The Goal
- ☐ Atomic Habits
- ☐ Leadership Pain
- ☐ _____
- ☐ _____
- ☐ _____
- ☐ _____
- ☐ _____
- ☐ _____

Application: what was interesting?

What did you do with the information? (Action required)

What was your AHA moment? (Didn't get one? Re-read it or give an explination why)

Book Specific Homework written out:

Journal Prompts

Exercises

What hope did you find?

Do you recommend this book to someone else? (circle one)

1   2   3   4   5   6   7   8   9   10
not at all   absolutely

Why?

Any suggestions for the therapy team?

COPYWRITE 2022 JOSHUA HOLLOWAY

Therapy BookIt!

Which book did you read?
- [ ] Gap and Gain
- [ ] Extreme Ownership
- [ ] Suffering
- [ ] The Goal
- [ ] Atomic Habits
- [ ] Leadership Pain
- [ ] _____
- [ ] _____
- [ ] _____
- [ ] _____
- [ ] _____
- [ ] _____

Application: what was interesting?

What did you do with the information? (Action required)

What was your AHA moment? (Didn't get one? Re-read it or give an explination why)

Book Specific Homework written out:

Journal Prompts

Exercises

What hope did you find?

Do you recommend this book to someone else? (circle one)

1   2   3   4   5   6   7   8   9   10
not at all   absolutely

Why?

Any suggestions for the therapy team?

COPYWRITE 2022 JOSHUA HOLLOWAY

Therapy BookIt!

Which book did you read?
- Gap and Gain
- Extreme Ownership
- Suffering
- The Goal
- Atomic Habits
- Leadership Pain
- _____
- _____
- _____
- _____
- _____
- _____

Application: what was interesting?

What did you do with the information? (Action required)

What was your AHA moment? (Didn't get one? Re-read it or give an explination why)

Book Specific Homework written out:

Journal Prompts

Exercises

What hope did you find?

Do you recommend this book to someone else? (circle one)

1   2   3   4   5   6   7   8   9   10
not at all   absolutely

Why?

Any suggestions for the therapy team?

COPYWRITE 2022 JOSHUA HOLLOWAY

Therapy BookIt!

Which book did you read?
- Gap and Gain
- Extreme Ownership
- Suffering
- The Goal
- Atomic Habits
- Leadership Pain
- _____
- _____
- _____
- _____
- _____
- _____

Application: what was interesting?

What did you do with the information? (Action required)

What was your AHA moment? (Didn't get one? Re-read it or give an explination why)

Book Specific Homework written out:

Journal Prompts

Exercises

What hope did you find?

Do you recommend this book to someone else? (circle one)

1   2   3   4   5   6   7   8   9   10
not at all   absolutely

Why?

Any suggestions for the therapy team?

COPYWRITE 2022 JOSHUA HOLLOWAY

Therapy BookIt!

Which book did you read?
- [ ] Gap and Gain
- [ ] Extreme Ownership
- [ ] Suffering
- [ ] The Goal
- [ ] Atomic Habits
- [ ] Leadership Pain
- [ ] _____
- [ ] _____
- [ ] _____
- [ ] _____
- [ ] _____
- [ ] _____

Application: what was interesting?

What did you do with the information? (Action required)

What was your AHA moment? (Didn't get one? Re-read it or give an explination why)

Book Specific Homework written out:

Journal Prompts

Exercises

What hope did you find?

Do you recommend this book to someone else? (circle one)

1   2   3   4   5   6   7   8   9   10
not at all   absolutely

Why?

Any suggestions for the therapy team?

COPYWRITE 2022 JOSHUA HOLLOWAY

Team Meeting Forms

Team Meeting

Meeting #:

Acceptance: to acknowledge what has happened to us that we had no control over

Ownership: what our personal behavior has produced for us in life

Goal: a measurable and achievable desire

Outcome: what the process produced

Insight on circumstances in the session

Actionable item for the Team Captain

COPYWRITE 2022 JOSHUA HOLLOWAY

Team Meeting

Meeting #:

Acceptance: to acknowledge what has happened to us that we had no control over

Ownership: what our personal behavior has produced for us in life

Goal: a measurable and achievable desire

Outcome: what the process produced

Insight on circumstances in the session

Actionable item for the Team Captain

COPYWRITE 2022 JOSHUA HOLLOWAY

Team Meeting

Meeting #:

Acceptance: to acknowledge what has happened to us that we had no control over

Ownership: what our personal behavior has produced for us in life

Goal: a measurable and achievable desire

Outcome: what the process produced

Insight on circumstances in the session

Actionable item for the Team Captain

Team Meeting

Meeting #:

Acceptance: to acknowledge what has happened to us that we had no control over

Ownership: what our personal behavior has produced for us in life

Goal: a measurable and achievable desire

Outcome: what the process produced

Insight on circumstances in the session

Actionable item for the Team Captain

COPYWRITE 2022 JOSHUA HOLLOWAY

Team Meeting

Meeting #:

Acceptance: to acknowledge what has happened to us that we had no control over

Ownership: what our personal behavior has produced for us in life

Goal: a measurable and achievable desire

Outcome: what the process produced

Insight on circumstances in the session

Actionable item for the Team Captain

COPYWRITE 2022 JOSHUA HOLLOWAY

Team Meeting

Meeting #:

Acceptance: to acknowledge what has happened to us that we had no control over

Ownership: what our personal behavior has produced for us in life

Goal: a measurable and achievable desire

Outcome: what the process produced

Insight on circumstances in the session

Actionable item for the Team Captain

COPYWRITE 2022 JOSHUA HOLLOWAY

Team Meeting

Meeting #:

Acceptance: to acknowledge what has happened to us that we had no control over

Ownership: what our personal behavior has produced for us in life

Goal: a measurable and achievable desire

Outcome: what the process produced

Insight on circumstances in the session

Actionable item for the Team Captain

COPYWRITE 2022 JOSHUA HOLLOWAY

Team Meeting

Meeting #:

Acceptance: to acknowledge what has happened to us that we had no control over

Ownership: what our personal behavior has produced for us in life

Goal: a measurable and achievable desire

Outcome: what the process produced

Insight on circumstances in the session

Actionable item for the Team Captain

COPYWRITE 2022 JOSHUA HOLLOWAY

Team Meeting

Meeting #:

Acceptance: to acknowledge what has happened to us that we had no control over

Ownership: what our personal behavior has produced for us in life

Goal: a measurable and achievable desire

Outcome: what the process produced

Insight on circumstances in the session

Actionable item for the Team Captain

COPYWRITE 2022 JOSHUA HOLLOWAY

Team Meeting

Meeting #:

Acceptance: to acknowledge what has happened to us that we had no control over

Ownership: what our personal behavior has produced for us in life

Goal: a measurable and achievable desire

Outcome: what the process produced

Insight on circumstances in the session

Actionable item for the Team Captain

COPYWRITE 2022 JOSHUA HOLLOWAY

Team Meeting

Meeting #:

Acceptance: to acknowledge what has happened to us that we had no control over

Ownership: what our personal behavior has produced for us in life

Goal: a measurable and achievable desire

Outcome: what the process produced

Insight on circumstances in the session

Actionable item for the Team Captain

COPYWRITE 2022 JOSHUA HOLLOWAY

Team Meeting

Meeting #:

Acceptance: to acknowledge what has happened to us that we had no control over

Ownership: what our personal behavior has produced for us in life

Goal: a measurable and achievable desire

Outcome: what the process produced

Insight on circumstances in the session

Actionable item for the Team Captain

COPYWRITE 2022 JOSHUA HOLLOWAY

Notes

Notes

Notes